Soulstepping

Soulstepping

African American Step Shows

Elizabeth C. Fine

University of Illinois Press
Urbana and Chicago

Publication of this book was supported by a grant
from Virginia Polytechnic Institute and State University.

Library of Congress Cataloging-in-Publication Data
Fine, Elizabeth C. (Elizabeth Calvert)
Soulstepping : African American step shows / Elizabeth C. Fine.
p. cm.
Includes bibliographical references and index.
ISBN 0-252-02475-3 (cloth : alk. paper)
1. African American dance—History.
2. Greek letter societies—History.
I. Title.
GV1624.7.A34F56   2003
793.3'089'96073—dc21   2002004789

To all the soulsteppers, past and present,
whose dedication to excellence has developed this art
to its highest form.

Contents

Acknowledgments

When I first attended an African American step show in 1984, little did I imagine that steppers would someday be invited to perform for the inauguration festivities of a U.S. president or that so many schools, churches, community groups, and other Greek-letter societies would also form step teams. Although I have tried to document this rapid growth and change, the stepping "movement" is developing in so many different directions and places that it is hard for any one book to embrace them all. The First National Conference on Stepping, held in Blacksburg, Virginia, on 6–7 April 2001, after this manuscript was under review, brought me in contact with still more organizations that are using stepping to effect social change. There, Patricia M. Mason from the Greater Rochester Step-Off explained how her nonprofit organization in New York uses stepping to mentor youth, and Jerry Smith of In-Step, Inc., told of his stepping program that helps at-risk youths in south Florida. Later, I met Haris Hardaway, founder of the Greater Boston Step Association, which uses stepping in a multifaceted program of cultural education and leadership building among young people. No doubt many more people are developing and transforming stepping to serve new audiences and purposes. I hope this book will open the door for others who will continue to examine the ever-changing and innovative tradition of stepping.

I owe an enormous debt of gratitude to the many people who so generously and enthusiastically shared their knowledge about stepping with me. To all of those persons interviewed in this book, my sincerest thanks for sharing your knowledge and experiences with me. Without you, this book would not have been possible. A number of persons deserve special thanks . for their great help. I am deeply grateful to my former student, Johna W. Robinson Vazquez, who started me on this journey by inviting me to a step show at Virginia Polytechnic Institute and State University (Virginia Tech) in 1984. She helped me understand different types of steps and the world of African American Greek-letter societies.

Richard Schechner encouraged the writing of my first essay on stepping, "Stepping, Saluting, Cracking, and Freaking: The Cultural Politics of African American Step Shows," for *The Drama Review* in 1991. Parts of chapters 2 and 5 first appeared there, and I thank MIT Press Journals for permission to reprint portions of it. I also thank the National Endowment for the Humanities for providing a summer stipend in 1995 for research at Howard University, and Dean Robert Bates at Virginia Tech, who supported this project with a College of Arts and Sciences Research Assignment in 1999 and a millennium grant in 2000. The Rylsky Institute gave permission to reprint parts of my paper "Oral-Formulaic Composition of African American Stepping," presented at the Oral Epic Conference in Kiev, parts of which appear in chapter 5. I am grateful to Clifford L. Muse, Jr., of the Moorland-Spingarn Research Center, Howard University, for his help in reprinting the photographs from the Howard University yearbooks and the Hampton University Museum and Archives for information on Reuben T. Caluza and permission to reprint a photograph of the African Quartette. I am especially grateful to my editor Judith McCulloh, who believed in this project and nurtured it from the beginning, and to my copy editor, Mary Giles. I greatly appreciate Jerrilyn McGregory and Wilsonia Cherry for their careful reading and astute comments on the manuscript, which made this a better book.

Dwayne Dixon gave me helpful advice and encouragement along the way and introduced me to other leaders in the National Pan-Hellenic Council. Michael K. Herndon and Ann Kilkelly read earlier versions of the manuscript and led me to other sources. Colleagues at the International Colloquium on Communication provided critical insight to parts of this book that were presented as papers in San Francisco in 1996 and in Boston in 2000. B'Jordan Brookins, Stephon D. Henderson, Robert J. Cummings, and Allison Cotton enriched my experience at Howard University with their enthusiasm and help. Linda Plaut musically notated several steps, and Kent Holliday scored these notations on a computer. Walter M. Kimbrough, Darryl R. Matthews, Sr., and Michael V. W. Gordon shared experience and insights on black Greek life. Pamela Middleton introduced me to the religious stepping of the Oak Grove A.M.E. Church, in Detroit, Michigan, and Fredrick Scott sent his excellent videos of the Oak Grove A.M.E. steppers. Tanoah Morgan led me to "A Christian Step Show and FUN-draiser" in Washington, D.C., where Tyrone C. Petty and David H. Smith helped me understand Christian stepping. Brian Williams, Paul Woodruff, and Jeff Johnson from Step Afrika! provided great encouragement as well as information, and

Tamer Mokhtar shared knowledge of stepping in Omega Psi Phi fraternity. Anthony Aldaño introduced me to stepping in Latino Greek fraternities and sororities, and Nihar Kulkarni helped me understand stepping in his Asian-interest fraternity, Alpha Iota Omicron.

I am also grateful to Sadie Allen, Carol D. Branch, Benjamin Dixon, Calvin Jamison, Darrell Hairston, Mary Mills, Grace Okrah, Eric Peterson, Judy Roby, Sarah Sprague, and Rose Laignel for their help. A very special thanks to my husband, Hazen Robert Walker, who edited many manuscript drafts and photographed and videotaped many step shows, and to our daughter, Grace Walker, for her assistance in recording step shows. I am grateful to them both for their patience during the long process of writing this book.

Introduction

I said, "Your mama didn't tell you 'bout **A Phi A?**
She didn't tell you 'bout the brothers and their sexy ways?
She didn't tell you how they slide to the side so sweet?
She didn't tell you 'bout the first of all black Greeks?
She didn't put you on her knee and break it on down?
Uh Uh Uh Uh **A PHI A!**"
—Alpha Phi Alpha Fraternity, Inc., Virginia Tech, 1983

When I was a middle-class white child growing up in the 1950s and 1960s, my mama never told me about "A Phi A." Alpha Phi Alpha was the first African American fraternity organized on a college campus. I never pledged a sorority or dated a fraternity man; indeed, my friends in the late 1960s viewed fraternities and sororities as elitist. Although I attended integrated universities, I had never seen any black fraternities and sororities. When an African American student in my class on verbal art invited me to a block show on the Virginia Tech campus in 1983, I had no idea what blocking or stepping was. Late in the afternoon, I joined a large crowd of predominantly black students to watch black fraternities and sororities express love for their Greek-letter societies through a complex performance involving synchronized percussive movement, singing, speaking, chanting, and drama. I was astounded by the power and energy of the performances, the creativity, and the enthusiastic audience response. Performing intricate stomps and claps, with chants that extolled their organizations' virtues or criticized rival organizations, the costumed performers captivated the audience with their vitality. Audience members would cheer on their favorite organizations, yell out club calls such as "skee wee" or "nupe, nupe," laugh, and shout. Later, when I told European American friends about the performance and asked if any had ever seen one, they all said no; they had never even heard of it.

That was not surprising because the university of around twenty-two thousand had only a small percentage of African American students in 1983. The informal step show was advertised by word of mouth and performed for a largely black student audience. Although a more public and larger step show had been organized in 1983 as a scholarship fund-raiser, it was too new to have attracted the attention of the larger community.

Had I been a college-bound African American student, however, I most certainly would have heard about historically black fraternities and sororities such as Alpha Phi Alpha or Delta Sigma Theta. The nine historically black Greek-letter societies have served, since their beginning in the early 1900s, as important social networks and leadership training grounds for African Americans. Leaders and artists such as Supreme Court Justice Thurgood Marshall, Martin Luther King, Jesse Jackson, Andrew Young, Marion Barry, Tom Bradley, Shirley Chisholm, Julian Bond, Mary McLeod Bethune, Barbara Jordan, Nikki Giovanni, Paula Giddings, Dionne Warwick, Langston Hughes, Zora Neale Hurston, George Washington Carver, James Weldon Johnson, and Carter G. Woodson are but a few of the many distinguished people who joined either undergraduate or graduate chapters. Black Greek-letter organizations proudly identify an estimated 75 percent of the black leaders in business, government, science, and the arts as alumni of their organizations.[1]

These organizations have worked on both local and national levels for social changes that have benefited not just African Americans but all Americans. From improving health care, raising scholarship funds, and promoting literacy to working for women's rights, aiding the NAACP, and organizing for social justice and civil rights, black Greek-letter organizations have been a major force for social action in America. Many who pledge while undergraduates continue to be active in graduate chapters that promote a life-long commitment to such ideals as scholarship, leadership, perseverance, service, and uplift.

Today African American step shows are much more visible than they were in the 1980s. Seen in films, television programs, advertisements, a syndicated step competition on the World African Network, and now in elementary, middle, and high schools, housing projects, and churches, this dynamic and rapidly changing art form has attracted an array of new audiences and performers. Members of college, alumni, and overseas chapters of African American Greek organizations are finding new venues for their ritual dances. A Ukrainian high school student in an American school in Brussels reports that she and her friends have learned to step, and dance ethnographer Jacqui Malone calls stepping "one of the most exciting dance forms to evolve in the twentieth century."[2]

What makes stepping so stimulating is the range of movement patterns and verbal genres it encompasses. The combination of speaking, chanting, and singing, along with stomping, clapping, gymnastics, and choreographed movements, creates a reflexive, malleable, and highly expressive art form. Very old patterns deriving from slave culture and Africa mix with modern influences such as break dancing, drill teams, and rap to whirl the spectator through an electrifying mixture of African American culture. "Stepping is tap dancing without tap shoes, James Brown without the music of the JB's, Cab Calloway sans piano, a marching band without John Philip Sousa. It is jazz, funk, rhythm and blues, and rap without instruments," says *Washington Post* writer Jill Nelson.[3]

Stepping is also exciting because it is reflexive, able to preserve and tell part of its history through one type of step called a "retrospect." A retrospect might recount details about the founding of a fraternity or sorority as well as celebrate favorite steps from the past by performing them in a medley. While steppers respect tradition and keep "signature" or "trade" steps alive, they constantly innovate, bending the old to serve the new and in the process creating the unexpected. The verbal component of stepping allows participants to speak in a particularly powerful way. Whether it is to shout and stomp out their group's name, impart a political or spiritual message, sing their own praises, or humorously put down rival groups, the combination of stylized verbal and movement patterns creates an unusually powerful rhetoric.

Stepping originated on college campuses among black fraternities and sororities as a ritual dance performance known variously as "stepping," "blocking," "hopping," "demonstrating," and "marching." These complex performances involve various combinations of singing, speaking, chanting, and synchronized movement. Fundamentally, stepping is a ritual performance of group identity. It expresses an organization's spirit, style, icons, and unity. Stepping also is a vibrant arena for the display of African American verbal and nonverbal art, because performers craft their routines from such black folk traditions and communicative patterns as call and response, rapping, the dozens, signifying, marking, spirituals, handclap games, and military chants, mixing them with tunes and images from popular culture into a relatively new performance tradition.

Approximately 1.5 million people belonged to the undergraduate and graduate chapters of the nine historically black Greek-letter organizations affiliated with the National Pan-Hellenic Council (NPHC) in 1999.[4] Many of these members participate in step shows, as either performers or audience members. If one were to count the step teams of other black organizations, schools, communities, and churches, as well as those in Latino, Asian, and multicultural fraternities and sororities, the number of people participating in step shows would expand considerably. Yet until more recent television and film recordings of stepping, such as in the opening pageant of the 1996 Summer Olympics, Spike Lee's film *School Daze* (1988), the nationally televised *S.T.O.M.P.* (*Step Out National Championships*, first shown in 1992), and the television situation comedy *A Different World*, few persons outside of the African American community had seen step shows.

Students who join a black Greek-letter organization participate in a major ritual of status transformation and elevation. Membership represents access to a network that can play a vital social role, not only in the college years but also throughout life. To establish and maintain a unique black Greek identity, each fraternity and sorority must define itself with symbols and styles that distinguish it from any other group. Indeed, members first learn to step as part of their initiation process and are often encouraged to perform publicly as a sign of their new status. Step shows have become a key venue for displaying and asserting group identity as well as for negotiating the status of each group within the social order. Among non-Greek organizations, stepping also functions as a ritual of group identity.

Despite its increasing prominence and the creativity, intelligence, wit, and physical skill displayed in this rich tradition, stepping has received little formal study. Few black Greek organizations mention stepping in their official published histories, which focus on organizational development and accomplishments. Because black Greek-letter societies dedicate themselves to uplifting and strengthening African American communities through work on a wide variety of social and economic projects, the serious work of social activism has taken precedence over documenting their stepping traditions. Although I will be mentioning some of the noteworthy accomplishments of these groups, my focus will be on the rich tradition of stepping. A comprehensive look at the history and social service accomplishments of the nine Greek-letter societies composing the NPHC appears in Lawrence C. Ross's *The Divine Nine.*[5]

In the first published scholarly research on the phenomenon, "Stepping, Saluting, Cracking, and Freaking: The Cultural Politics of African-American Step Shows," I defined stepping, explored some of its American and African folk roots, and discussed the effects of institutionalized competitions on the cultural politics and style of stepping. In *Steppin' on the Blues: The Visible Rhythms of African American Dance,* Jacqui Malone devotes the final chapter to stepping, identifying its roots in African and African American dance traditions and discussing stepping at Howard University. Although

Malone does an excellent job of discussing the dance traditions upon which stepping draws, her coverage of stepping is limited to the college/university arena and focused tightly on Howard University. Further, because she makes no use of the rich visual record of stepping that emerges in the Howard University yearbook, *The Bison,* she does not discuss the evolution of stepping styles that the pictorial history and commentary reveals. Articles by Amy Davis, Alicia J. Rouverol, and Lisa J. Yarger further probe the effects of competition on stepping; discuss the aesthetics of "hot," "cool," and "getting down"; and explore Afrocentricity and beliefs about stepping at the University of North Carolina. A number of articles in the popular press, including *Rolling Stone* and *The Wall Street Journal,* document the increasing spread and influence of stepping.[6]

One reason that stepping has received so little study lies in a well-documented bias in Western criticism against critical studies of dance. In her masterful book *Body, Movement, and Culture,* Sally Ann Ness reviews the reasons for this devaluation of dance and movement studies. Euro-American criticism tends to view dance phenomena as "natural," products of intuitive or unconscious feelings that require little if any interpretation, according to Susan Leigh Foster. Ness links this attitude to deeply ingrained negative attitudes toward the body and bodily experiences in general, citing a number of important works that discuss the body "as a problematized, anxiety-ridden concept in Euro-American worldviews." Influenced by Cynthia J. Novack's *Sharing the Dance,* Ness attempts to "return bodily experience *as a form of consciousness and understanding* to a central place within the discipline of ethnographic inquiry." Just as one may "read" material and verbal culture, one can "read" nonverbal culture: "even the simplest gesture can make visible a culture's most cherished and carefully shaped relationships."[7]

Soulstepping attempts to "read" the varied phenomena of stepping through detailed ethnographic observations of various step shows as well as interviews with participants. In contrast to earlier studies, this book includes interviews with people from a variety of college campuses as well as with steppers and stepping coaches from schools, churches, and dance groups. *Soulstepping* is a product of the many practitioners of the art of stepping and members of African American fraternities and sororities who patiently answered my many questions and shared their perspectives with me. In order to make sure that I quoted them accurately, whenever possible I sent them rough drafts of the manuscript for their review. Because it is important to honor the art and history of stepping by acknowledging the people who practice it, I have used the real names of those interviewed, except for a few who wished to remain anonymous.

Late one afternoon in 1995, when I was sitting on the steps of the Howard University Library waiting for a cab, I struck up a conversation with a black man about my age who was also waiting for a ride. He asked what I was doing at the library, and I told him about the book I was writing on stepping. With a smile, he said, "No offense or anything, but shouldn't you be writing a book about polka?" He went on to ask if I could step myself, and after I performed a few measures of Alpha Kappa Alpha's step "It's a Serious Matter," he said, "OK, I just wanted to see if you were for real." We went on to have a lively conversation, because he had been a tap dancer and choreographer before he entered the ministry.

Because all of the historically black fraternities and sororities accept members of all races, it is common to see a few white steppers. Indeed, when "The Unknown Step Team," composed of Phi Beta Sigma alumni, performed at the 1999 Philadelphia Greek Picnic Step Show, the three team members who actually stepped that evening were white. All of the persons I interviewed were very patient and helpful in helping me understand the culture of their fraternities and sororities. As Ann Cooper Albright, a white dance critic who has written extensively about African American dance says, "Being white is no excuse for not making the effort to learn about and come to understand the complexities and multiple layers of meaning in contemporary African-American epic dance."[8]

Studying this performance tradition sheds light on what James Clifford calls "the predicament of culture" in the modern and postmodern world. In the contemporary world of multinationalism and global travel and communication, this cultural predicament stems from constant interaction among different cultures. With the homogenization and cultural leveling of the "global village," cultural identities become fluid and negotiable. In response to tensions caused by rapid cultural change, persons often construct identities through syncretic performances that combine traditions of the past with contemporary cultural expressions. African American stepping has arisen out of the cultural displacement experienced by black students who have left their vernacular culture of home to attend college. As these students became integrated into predominantly white colleges and universities, the threat to their cultural identity became even more pronounced.[9]

The shift from the old-style circular stepping of the 1940s and 1950s to the increasingly complex synchronized movement style of the 1980s and 1990s attests to the new role stepping has played in asserting black cultural identity. The increasing visibility of step shows to non-Greek and non-African American audiences corresponds to the proud assertion of African American identity in American culture and to the popularity of hip-hop culture. But steppers do not simply repeat traditional verbal and nonverbal forms such as spirituals or handclap games; they recraft and meld them with contemporary sounds, movements, and issues. Stepping is a pliable form of communication that is taking new shapes to meet new purposes. While some might make its eye-catching, ear-arresting rhythms into showy, crowd-pleasing entertainment for the 1996 Summer Olympics, others are turning it into religious catechism and liturgy.

In discussing the development and transformation of African American stepping, I consider the cultural phenomenon from a variety of angles, beginning with its roots in African American fraternities and sororities. Because the various histories of the NPHC member organizations examine the accomplishments of these groups in depth, and because the development of stepping is complex in its own right, this book does not provide a detailed history of these societies. Starting with the first written and photographic coverage of stepping in the Howard University yearbook and student newspaper, chapter 1 examines seven decades of published records at Howard University. Although the history of stepping varies from campus to campus, interviews with students, faculty, and staff at Howard, along with analysis of journalistic coverage of stepping there and elsewhere, helps trace the evolution of stepping from a fraternity pledging ritual to a popular performance tradition.[10]

Chapter 2, "A Ritual Dance of Identity," probes deeper into the roots of stepping in fraternal and sororal pledging and initiation rituals, examining stepping as both a ritual process and an oral tradition. Stepping's role in transforming individual pledges into a brotherhood or sisterhood has grown in importance, particularly after the NPHC abolished pledging, replacing it with the "intake process" in 1990. Victor Turner's ritual stages of "liminality," when neophytes are "betwixt and between established roles and customs," and "communitas," in which they experience intense feelings of unity, manifest themselves in the probate shows of new pledges.[11] Chapter 2 also looks at stepping's role in the social drama of black Greek life and at festivals such as the annual Philadelphia Greek Picnic. Finally, it shows how stepping both reflects and creates cultural identity.

Because steppers are also quite conscious of celebrating their African roots, chapter 3 discusses the African and African American movement traditions that emerge in step shows. The chapter explores the claim made by some that stepping originated in South African gumboot dancing. It also examines the similarities between stepping and such early African American dances as ring shouts and patting juba. Using examples from a wide range of step shows, the chapter demonstrates how aesthetic features most prominent in African dance are also prominent in stepping.

Although stepping began among the first African American Greek-letter societies, other black organizations also engage in stepping. Sweetheart and support organizations of the nine national societies, as well as newer, non-traditional black societies such as Groove Phi Groove and Wine Psi Phi, perform in step shows on college campuses.[12] Elementary, middle, and high school children have formed step teams, as have church and community groups. Chapter 4, "Stepping Forth: New Participants and Venues," traces the movement of stepping from college events to off-campus sites and to Latino, Asian, and multicultural Greek-letter societies. It also discusses the factors that have led to greatly expanded audiences for stepping in the 1990s, exploring the impact of the shift from private to public audiences on the performance tradition itself. Probing the use of stepping as religious liturgy and ritual, the chapter includes interviews with leaders of the Oak Grove African Methodist Episcopal Church Steppers in Detroit, Michigan; participants in the Marsha Sumner Christian Step Show in Washington, D.C.; and the founders of Alpha Omega Alpha, a Christian fraternity that uses stepping in its ministry. Interviews with the Blacksburg High School Black Awareness Club Steppers in Blacksburg, Virginia, the coach of the Gamma Beta Tau Step Club in Fort Worth, Texas, and a coach of the AAMEN Steppers from St. Francis Xavier School in Washington, D.C., reveal how stepping serves the needs of elementary and secondary school children. Conversations with the producer of the television program *S.T.O.M.P.*, participants at the first intercollegiate Latino Greek step show in New York City, members of Asian American fraternities and sororities, and Step Afrika! (an international arts organization) show how stepping has been adapted to a broad range of new contexts and audiences. Because stepping is an oral tradition, steppers frequently use techniques of oral-formulaic composition to create new steps. They also use visual formulas and themes. Chapter 4 examines how persons create new steps by adapting formulas and themes to new contexts.

Although stepping has become more and more visible, it is by no means without its critics, both within and without Greek-letter organizations. Because not all African Americans like Greek-letter societies, and some, such as E. Franklin Frazier, have been highly critical of them, it is not surprising to find strong disagreements about stepping.[13] Some members of black Greek organizations feel that the popularity of stepping is causing both members and nonmembers alike to lose sight of their original missions. Further, because non-Greeks and non-blacks are beginning to step, some members of black Greek organizations are contesting the rights of others to adopt their traditional expressive art. As stepping has become commodified as a money-making event, new pressures and constraints have emerged. Should an Asian American fraternity be allowed to step on the nationally televised show *S.T.O.M.P,* or will that signal that African American Greek organizations are losing control of a vital tradition? Stepping is becoming so popular that the historically black fraternities and sororities risk being identified only with stepping, with the public losing sight of their social and charitable contributions. "Cracking," a popular form of stepping in which one group pokes fun at another, is seen by some as counterproductive in large, public fundraising shows. Chapter 5 takes up such issues in a discussion of "The Cultural Politics of African American Step Shows." The epilogue considers the implications of the dramatic growth in popularity of stepping on our understanding of the "cultural predicament" of African Americans and other minorities at the dawn of the twenty-first century.

Soulstepping explores the process of creating and negotiating identity through stepping, probing the intersections of verbal and nonverbal performances as well as issues of cultural politics and the effects of commodification. It is my hope that *Soulstepping* will be significant to the fields of dance, folklore, black studies, performance studies, communication, and to all those who are drawn to the beauty and power of African American stepping.

Because stepping is a feast for both eye and ear, photographs and video have played an important part in my analysis. The accompanying photographs, drawn from my own collection as well as the archives of the Moorland-Spingarn Research Center, capture some of the important details and developments in the evolution of stepping.

1 / A History of Stepping

Nineteen-o-eight was our founding date.
In '74 we did it once more.
Saying, "What? What?"
It's a serious matter.
Saying, "What? What?"
It's a serious matter.
—Alpha Kappa Alpha Sorority, Inc., Virginia Tech, 1986

People give widely varying answers to the simple question of when and where stepping began. Some say that they have always stepped and that stepping goes back to Africa. Others relate stepping to the fraternity and sorority pledging ritual of marching on line and date it to the 1940s.[1] While movement and communication patterns from African cultures are clearly evident in stepping, college students forged it out of their rich African American performance heritage of dance, speech, and song.

The development of stepping varies from one campus to another. National and regional meetings of the Greek-letter societies, however, fostered the exchange of steps and styles and the evolution of a common tradition within each. The best place to find information on how stepping developed in a college setting is to examine the written record at Howard University, birthplace of five of the nine black Greek-letter organizations. The excitement and controversy of stepping at Howard led to its documentation in student yearbooks and newspapers. Because the writers and photographers are Howard students, they provide an insider's viewpoint. These publications offer a sustained view of Greek life and ritual that is more comprehensive than the experience of any one informant. Thus they generate varying points of inquiry and are a corrective and supplement to oral histories. Before reviewing this coverage, however, we must examine the social context within which the first black Greek-letter societies developed.

The Development of Black Greek-letter Societies

Students who organized the first black Greek-letter societies in the early 1900s were experiencing a profound "cultural predicament," James Clifford's term for what happens to identities undergoing rapid cultural change and interacting with other, quite different, cultures. In such situations the idea of an authentic culture with clear-cut boundaries and traditions gives way to an emergent one, the product of interplay and appropriation among diverse groups. At the turn of the twentieth century, the black students who attended white colleges and universities in the North experienced social and cultural isolation. From segregated housing to segregated social clubs, African Americans were denied the kinds of support that European American students enjoyed. Further, their own social identities as African Americans were suppressed. At Cornell University, the social climate for black students was so unsupportive that "the six African American students from the 1904–05 class" did not enroll for the 1905–6 year.[2]

In response to this cultural suppression, seven black men at predominantly white Cornell University formed the first historically black Greek-letter fraternity, Alpha Phi Alpha, on 4 December 1906. Known as "the Seven Jewels," the founding members of Alpha Phi Alpha fraternity were strongly influenced by the social and political struggles at the end of the nineteenth and the beginning of the twentieth centuries, according to Charles Wesley. The Supreme Court's *Plessy v. Ferguson* decision in 1896 legalized "separate but equal" facilities for blacks and whites. Numerous other Jim Crow assaults on the rights of African Americans led to the Niagara Movement in 1905, one of the antecedents to the NAACP. During the "golden age of Negro secret societies" from 1890 to 1910, Malone notes, African Americans organized thousands of mutual aid societies to provide economic and social support to each other. As Alpha Phi Alpha founder Henry Arthur Callis said, "Society offered us narrowly circumscribed opportunity and no security. Out of our need, our fraternity brought social purpose and social action."[3]

The first initiation held by Alpha Phi Alpha occurred at the Masonic Hall, also known as Odd Fellows Hall and Red Men's Hall, after the students broke into the Masons' lockers so "attire more suited to the purpose than civilian clothing might be secured." This close association with an African American Masonic society, even to the point of borrowing their ritual clothing, suggests that early fraternities and sororities may have modeled some of their rituals on those of other secret societies of the time. Because mutual aid societies were known for their competitive drill teams, as Malone observes, it is possible that the black Greek-letter society tradition of marching on line, from which stepping likely evolved, may have been borrowed from such societies. Noting the popularity of drill teams in African American communities, Lawrence Ross says, "I would assume that stepping actually came from drill team movements."[4]

Those with Afrocentric philosophies may question why black students would imitate white Greek-letter organizations. Yet evidence suggests that these first college fraternal organizations gained much of their impetus from the great popularity of other African American mutual aid societies that flourished in eighteenth- and nineteenth-century America. Jacqui Malone argues persuasively that black Greek-letter societies "inherited a rich tradition of mutual aid and cultural reinforcement." She builds on Carter G. Woodson's 1936 argument that comparing mutual aid societies in Western Africa with leading African American ones would lead to significant results.[5]

During the years of Jim Crow racism, blacks had to keep many of their organized activities secret. Ismail Conway maintains that the students who organized the first black Greek-letter societies used an outward similarity to white Greek-letter societies to hide the more serious purpose of serving African American communities. In the climate of racism in which they began, argues Conway, it would have been difficult for such students to get permission from their colleges to organize a social club that had the word *African* in its name. At its fourth annual convention, held in 1911, Wesley notes that Alpha Phi Alpha fraternity appointed a committee "to do research work, especially as to the relation of the Ethiopian of ancient times to the black race of modern times." Thus, from its earliest years in existence Alpha Phi Alpha has demonstrated strong interest in African culture.[6]

Most authorities at black institutions of higher learning objected to their students forming Greek-letter societies, which, they believed, promoted "artificial caste and class distinctions." But the situation at Howard University in Washington, D.C., was different. Free from the control of church boards and white philanthropy, Howard received funds from the federal government. In 1907 the Beta chapter of Alpha Phi Alpha fraternity organized at Howard with nineteen students, becoming the first Greek-letter society at a black college or university. During the next thirteen years, six more Greek-letter societies organized at Howard. The first sorority, Alpha Kappa Alpha, started in 1908, followed by Delta Sigma Theta sorority, which split from it in 1913, and Zeta Phi Beta sorority in 1920. The second black fraternity, Omega Psi Phi, began at Howard in 1911, and the third fraternity, Phi Beta Sigma, organized in 1914. Kappa Alpha Psi fraternity began at Indiana University in 1911 under the leadership of two Howard transfer students and organized a chapter at Howard University in 1920.

Sigma Gamma Rho sorority began at Butler University in Indianapolis and at the Normal School at Terre Haute, Indiana, in 1922. It organized a chapter at Howard University in 1939.[7]

In 1930 members of black Greek-letter societies organized a national coordinating group, the National Pan-Hellenic Council, which helps constituents schedule national meetings and workshops and establish local councils. It also works cooperatively with other "enabling groups," such as the National Black Leadership Roundtable, the National Coalition of Black Voter Participation, the NAACP, the Urban League, and the United Negro College Fund.[8]

From 1922 to 1996 it was common to refer to these organizations as the eight historically black Greek-letter societies. But following a constitutional amendment authorizing expansion in 1993, the National Pan-Hellenic Council officially accepted a new fraternity, Iota Phi Theta, into its ranks on 12 November 1996. Founded in 1963 at Morgan State College in Baltimore, Maryland, Iota Phi Theta now has 175 chapters (and colonies) and approximately fifteen thousand members.[9]

Although each of the nine fraternities and sororities composing the NPHC are predominantly and historically African American, the organizations are open to all students, regardless of racial or ethnic identity. In 1949 Alpha Kappa Alpha initiated its first two white women into its Washington, D.C., graduate chapter. The two said that they were interested in advancing the sorority's goals for racial integration and human rights, as well as in civic improvements for blacks of lower economic circumstances.[10]

In the years following World War I, member chapters of the NPHC spread to major, racially integrated research universities and to many southern historically black colleges. Many alumni chapters started as "'Civic and Service' organizations" during this period, Ross notes, because "blatant racism prohibited African Americans from participating in general civic organizations in their communities after graduation from college." More chapters were organized at historically black colleges after World War II, and after desegregation in the 1960s the numbers of chapters that organized at white colleges and universities grew dramatically.[11]

Since their inception, the nine black Greek-letter organizations have played an important role in the civic and social health of American communities. In 1913 Delta Sigma Theta sisters marched side by side with white women in the march for woman suffrage in Washington, D.C. All the organizations have numerous local and national initiatives. They support the NAACP, monitor national legislation, conduct literacy campaigns, register voters, improve housing and employment opportunities, support food and clothing banks, and mentor youths.[12]

Each of the nine Greek-letter organizations shares similar goals of scholarship, character, and community service. Yet each has its own distinctive personality. For example, members of Omega Psi Phi fraternity cultivate a powerful masculine style, calling themselves the "nasty Q-dogs." In contrast, Kappa Alpha Psi is proud of its debonair, playboy image. Alpha Kappa Alpha sisters are known for their ladylike demeanor, and Zeta Phi Beta sisters pride themselves on their ideal of "finer womanhood" and "grace under pressure."[13]

The historically black Greek-letter societies typify what Clifford calls "emergent culture."[14] They combine elements from both European American and African American Greek-letter societies and infuse their rituals with African American communication patterns and traditions.

Stepping is a quintessential emergent art form, a collage of old rhythms and movements melded with the new. Stepping bends the tunes of plaintive spirituals into hymns of fraternal/sororal devotion and praise. It mixes centuries-old movement patterns from African and slave dances, such as patting juba and ring shouts, with the percussive foot and hand movements of black cheerleaders and drill teams. Adding beats from the latest dances and musical hits, steppers blend old and new. Stepping has become a vehicle for showcasing the unique style of each fraternity and sorority, an important ritual of group identity, and an increasingly popular tool for schools, communities, and churches to mentor African American youths.

The 1920s and 1930s: Dancing to "the Fairy Pipes of Pan"

It is difficult to find written support for the existence of stepping before 1924, when the first yearbook and newspaper were published at Howard University. No pictures of Greek pledging activities appear in the *Bison* yearbook during the 1920s and 1930s. The earliest written reference to what might be stepping appears in the 25 November 1925 student newspaper, the *Hilltop*. In an article entitled "Hell-Week," Van Taylor described pledging activities of Omega Psi Phi and Kappa Alpha Psi fraternities: "What desire is this that will cause young men, stalwart of frame, and rugged of heart and mind, demurely and aesthetically to dance about the campus as if in time to the fairy Pipes of Pan?"[15] Hell Week, of course, is a colloquial expression for the intense pledge activities that probates must endure the week before they are accepted into a society. The phrase *fairy Pipes of Pan* suggests that the men are performing to a music or beat that only they can hear; in other words, there is no accompanying music. The word *demurely* suggests a certain restraint or gravity to their movements, as might befit initiates in a ritual; *aesthetically* suggests an artful quality to their movements. Within eighteen years of the formation of the first black Greek-letter society, a public ritual dance associated with pledging had developed.

Van Taylor's description of dancing young fraternity men may also be an account of the ritual performance of group identity called "marching on line," from which stepping evolved. During the pledge period, pledges ("probates") demonstrate their newfound brotherhood or sisterhood by walking together across campus, all wearing their group's colors and symbols and cultivating the same look, style, and movement. Explaining this ritual, a Howard University student writes that people walk in a line and "wear, eat, sleep, or think the same thing" in order to learn the concepts of "unity, trust, and devotion" and achieve closeness between the members of each organization.[16]

While cultivating group identity through ritual performance builds loyalty to the group, it can lead to intense rivalry among competing organizations. Two articles of the early 1930s discuss the role of the Inter-Fraternity Council in promoting unity among Greek-letter organizations. Both comment on the strong competition among the societies that was adversely affecting student life. According to the 1930 *Bison,* "The jousting for political preferment and social advantage, is so keen at times that there is no telling to what extremes, fraternities or unscrupulous members of fraternities will go to achieve these ends." By 1932, however, the *Bison* reported that the influence of the Inter-Fraternity Council had led these groups to "work and pull together . . . for their common good and the progress of the University."[17]

The 1940s and 1950s: "On Line" and "On Parade"

Pledging rituals photographed during the 1940s and 1950s reveal the linear formations of pledges marching on line. The first pictures of Greek activities appeared in the 1940s. The 1943 *Bison* included several unlabeled photographs of fraternity and sorority pledges on-line and a fraternity engaged in a public skit (fig. 1). Twelve young men in suits and ties, with dog collars and long chains around their necks, pose behind the university's sundial ("the Dial"), a traditional gathering spot for Omega Psi Phi (the "Q-Dogs"). The Omegas unofficially adopted the dog as their mascot (the mascot of Howard University before 1920 was a bulldog), and many members howled and used canine symbols. Two other groups of identically dressed men also appear to be pledges on line. One group holds stacks of books under their left arms as they pose in a pyramid formation. Each member of the other group holds a wrapped package (about the size of a brick) under his right arm. (These are probably Kappas, who carry bricks

Figure 1. The first pictures of Greek-letter societies at Howard University in public displays appeared in the 1943 *Bison*. (1943 Howard University *Bison*, p. 84, courtesy of the Moorland-Spingarn Research Center, Howard University Archives)

as one of their icons.) In still another photograph of a public skit, young men gather around a man who is on his knees and wearing a long, Egyptian-looking headdress, a common ritual costume of Alpha Phi Alpha. In one photograph, women, dressed alike, pose around baskets and a stuffed rabbit; in another, seven young women march in a line down a sidewalk, each with her hands on the hips of the girl in front of her. The woman in front calls over her shoulder to those behind. They might be stepping, because such formations are common in step routines. The 1947 *Bison* also shows the Omegas on line, again sporting dog collars and long chains but carrying lanterns.[18]

The visual record of probates on line increased dramatically in the *Bison* during the 1950s, and marching on line often involved singing or chanting and syncopated and synchronized movements. In 1950, nine out of the eleven photographs on two pages of "Campus Candids" reveal various unnamed sororities and fraternities on line. In the 1955 *Bison*, Kappa and AKA pledges march side by side on line, and Delta pledges on line carry pandas and either sing or chant. Identically dressed Omegas carry lanterns and sing or chant as they, too, march in a line. The 1957 *Bison* devotes a page to pictures of probates; those from AKA and Kappa Alpha Psi march across campus in a line, singing or chanting. The 1958 *Bison* features two pages of Greek activities, with photographs of Kappas marching and chanting or singing on line, and AKA and DST sorority probates "on Parade" (fig. 2). The probates of DST face each other in two long lines as each leans toward the woman across from her and sings. The caption reads "sing girls." Greek singing events also contributed to the musical and verbal components of stepping.[19]

The 1960s and 1970s: Greek Weekend, Demonstrations, and Greek Shows

In contrast to the linear patterns in photographs from the previous two decades, the circle was the most commonly photographed pattern in both singing and stepping rituals during the 1960s. During that decade, twenty-four photographs in the *Bison* revealed some type of singing or stepping. Fifteen were of groups in circles, with eight of these showing circular movement. Six of the eight indicated counterclockwise motion. Prevalent in African dance, the counterclockwise circular pattern seen in early step routines reflects the influence of African cultures. Such patterns echo the circular, counterclockwise pattern of the ring shout and patting juba, early African American dances (chapter 2). Two photographs in the 1964 *Bison* show AKA sorors standing and moving in a counterclockwise circle, with captions that read "Singing on Campus" (fig. 3) and "Hipp-O-Hi-O."[20] DST sisters

Figure 2. Stepping may have originated from pledging rituals such as marching on line. The "Plugs of AKA" demonstrate unity by marching on-line at Howard University. (1958 Howard University *Bison*, p. 95, courtesy of the Moorland-Spingarn Research Center, Howard University Archives)

encircle a tree as they sway side to side and sing (fig. 4). In a 1969 *Bison* photograph, Omega brothers demonstrate their lively "Omega Bop" as they kick and move in a counterclockwise circle around the Dial (fig. 5). AKA sorors also move counterclockwise during their "Friday Songtime" (fig. 6). Alpha Phi Alpha brothers step in a counterclockwise circle as they sing "Movin' on Up" at "the Fountain" (fig. 7).

The first photographs of a formalized indoor stepping program called "Greek Weekend" appeared in the 1965 *Bison*. The first annual Greek Weekend was organized in response to heightened criticism of Greek-letter societies on campuses and to a decreasing membership. The Weekend included six individual sessions on Greek life as well as "a colorful pledge club program in the auxiliary gym of the New Men's Gymnasium." In the first photograph of Greek Weekend, Alpha Phi Alpha pledges circle clockwise around a brother, and in the second, pledges of an unnamed sorority encircle a woman (figs. 8, 9). Students also perform such circular steps at the 1965

Figure 3. Marching and stepping in a counterclockwise circle, sorors demonstrate their sisterhood. (1964 Howard University *Bison*, p. 271, courtesy of the Moorland-Spingarn Research Center, Howard University Archives)

Figure 4. Delta Sigma Theta sorors sing around a tree at Howard University. (1964 Howard University *Bison*, p. 275, courtesy of the Moorland-Spingarn Research Center, Howard University Archives)

Figure 5. "Brothers demonstrate 'Omega Bop' for spectators." (1969 Howard University *Bison,* p. 221, courtesy of the Moorland-Spingarn Research Center, Howard University Archives)

Figure 6. "Sorors eagerly partici-pate in Friday Songtime at the AKA plot." (1969 Howard University *Bison,* p. 213, courtesy of the Moorland-Spingarn Research Center, Howard University Archives)

Figure 7. Alpha Phi Alpha brothers step in a counterclockwise circle as they sing at "the Fountain." (1970 Howard University *Bison*, p. 190, courtesy of the Moorland-Spingarn Research Center, Howard University Archives)

Figure 8. The 1965 Greek Weekend pledge group's program consisted of "skits and songs performed for the big brothers and big sisters." (1965 Howard University *Bison*, p. 207, courtesy of the Moorland-Spingarn Research Center, Howard University Archives)

Figure 9. Pledges perform for their big brothers and sisters during Greek Weekend at Howard University. (1965 Howard University *Bison,* p. 203, courtesy of the Moorland-Spingarn Research Center, Howard University Archives)

Greek Ball, where they snap their fingers as they move counterclockwise around a person performing in the center (fig. 10). In a closeup on the Omega Psi Phi page, members demonstrate some of the angular arm movements that are still part of stepping (fig. 11).[21]

A powerful closeup of two male probates in the 1966 *Bison* captures the solemnity of pledging rituals. Dressed in tuxedos, cravats, and top hats, they stand at attention, with solemn expressions typical of the demeanor expected of probates in this liminal phase of a rite of passage (fig. 12). Twenty-three other brothers stand with them, as a long shot of the complete v-shaped formation reveals.[22]

Photographs of the late 1960s showed both singing and stepping in Howard's Yard, although the term *stepping* is not used. The 1967 Omega Psi Phi page features a probate (fig. 13) who looks strikingly like the Omega probates in their 1995 probate show at Howard (fig. 14): bald heads, sunglasses, the Omega letter painted on their foreheads, carrying shields, their faces rigid with the same stoic expressions. Two photographs in the 1969 *Bison* portray fraternities singing. The Alphas lift their right feet in unison as they sing (fig. 15), and exuberant Kappa brothers raise their hands high as they sing around their tree (fig. 16).

Figure 10. At the Greek Ball, Howard University. (1965 Howard University *Bison*, p. 204, courtesy of the Moorland-Spingarn Research Center, Howard University Archives)

Figure 11. Omega Psi Phi brothers at Howard University. (1965 Howard University *Bison*, p. 213, courtesy of the Moorland-Spingarn Research Center, Howard University Archives)

Figure 12. Probates at Howard University. (1965 Howard University *Bison*, p. 166, courtesy of the Moorland-Spingarn Research Center, Howard University Archives)

Figure 13. The bald head and solemn facial expression on this probate at Howard University in 1967 is characteristic of the liminal phase of an Omega Psi Phi fraternity probate show. (1967 Howard University *Bison*, p. 234, courtesy of the Moorland-Spingarn Research Center, Howard University Archives)

Figure 14. Omega Psi Phi probates at Howard University, 1995. (Photograph by Elizabeth Fine)

Figure 15. Expressing intense community, Alpha Phi Alpha brothers at Howard University "sing with their new brothers" after "the pledge line goes over." (1969 Howard University *Bison*, p. 215, courtesy of the Moorland-Spingarn Research Center, Howard University Archives)

Figure 16. "The brothers break out in song around the Kappa Tree." (1969 Howard University *Bison*, p. 219, courtesy of the Moorland-Spingarn Research Center, Howard University Archives)

The words *demonstrate* and *demonstration* to describe stepping began to appear in campus periodicals in the 1960s. In a letter to the editor of the *Hilltop* in April 1964, Leroy E. Giles observed, "I noticed the recent demonstrations by the fraternities and sororities on campus. The pageantry and pomp gladdened, as always, the heart of this lover of parades." A 1969 *Bison* caption proclaimed, "Brothers demonstrate 'Omega Bop' for spectators on Fridays."[23]

Photographs of stepping and indoor step shows increased substantially in the 1970s. In most cases writers referred to stepping as a "demonstration." "Nearly fifty pledges leave campus after demonstrating," says a caption in the 1970 *Bison*. "A crowd gathers for the 'Que' demonstration on campus," states another. A 1973 *Hilltop* photograph of the Kappas stepping in the Yard refers to "Kappa-Stomping." But in 1974, for the first time, the *Bison* contained one page of photographs of an indoor step show with the heading "Greek Demonstration" (fig. 17).[24]

The words *The Demonstration* head two pages in the 1975 *Bison* that include photographs of stepping outside and in front of large audiences. Brothers (probably Kappas) step with striped canes (fig. 18), and an unnamed group of brothers dressed in Egyptian-style garb steps as they chant or sing (fig. 19). The group is probably Alpha Phi Alpha, which uses the

Sphinx as an icon and often wears such clothing to signify its identity with Africa. A line of five fashionably dressed sorors poses seductively in a model-like stance, and others adopt Afrocentric fashions in another uncaptioned photograph (figs. 20, 21).

After 1975 the word *demonstration* no longer appears in conjunction with stepping. A political demonstration held in October 1975 to protest the rising costs of education and demand a better bookstore and library facilities was described in the 1976 *Bison* under the heading "Campus Demonstration—

Figure 17. One of the first photographs of an indoor step show at Howard University. "Another part of Homecoming '73 included Greek Demonstrations. AKA's, Grooves, Deltas—all did their thing, as those present enjoyed the whole bit." (1974 Howard University *Bison*, p. 37, courtesy of the Moorland-Spingarn Research Center, Howard University Archives)

Figure 18. Canes are a trademark of Kappa Alpha Psi and, less commonly, of Phi Beta Sigma. (1975 Howard University *Bison*, p. 73, courtesy of the Moorland-Spingarn Research Center, Howard University Archives)

Figure 19. Brothers, probably Alphas, step. The page is captioned "The Demonstration." (1975 Howard University *Bison*, p. 73, courtesy of the Moorland-Spingarn Research Center, Howard University Archives)

Figure 20. Striking a model's stance in the Howard University Yard. (1975 Howard University *Bison*, p. 77, courtesy of the Moorland-Spingarn Research Center, Howard University Archives)

Figure 21. Sorors adopt an Afrocentric look in a "Demonstration." (1975 Howard University *Bison*, p. 77, courtesy of the Moorland-Spingarn Research Center, Howard University Archives)

Yesterday and Today." That may have helped shift the referent for the word to indicate direct political action rather than aesthetic and social events. Other stepping synonyms appeared in Kujaliwa Hukumu's 1976 letter critical of black Greeks: "shout'n foot stomp'n tribalism," a "war dance," and "marches."[25]

By the late 1970s, pictures of indoor step shows revealed large audiences and elaborate costumes. Malone notes that during this period the administration at Howard began scheduling noon classes, so stepping in the Yard began to decline slowly. Yet Greek shows of stepping gained in popularity, and by 1976 the first competitive Greek show was scheduled for homecoming week.[26]

The 1977 *Bison* includes several photographs of outdoor stepping. In five of them, the Sphinx Club (pledges of Alpha Phi Alpha) is on line and stepping. One photograph captures a common stepping stance seen in probate shows, in which the pledges perform in a squatting position (fig. 22). Such a posture not only symbolizes the lowly status of the pledges but also expresses the African "get-down quality," common in West and Central African dance, in which dancers crouch close to the ground in a virtuoso demonstration of honor and respect. In other photographs, on line AKA sisters

Figure 22. The Alpha Phi Alpha Sphinx Club performs in a squatting position. (1977 Howard University *Bison*, p. 124, courtesy of the Moorland-Spingarn Research Center, Howard University Archives)

are being reviewed by a senior soror and are outside, in a circle, arms inter-locked. In contrast, all the photographs of stepping in the 1978 and 1979 *Bison* are from indoor shows and reveal large audiences and elaborate cos-tumes—white tuxedos for the Kappas, black tuxedos for the Alphas, and matching calico western square-dancing dresses for AKA.[27]

The 1980s: "Steppin' Out" and "Showing Off"

Throughout the 1980s, stepping appeared with greater prominence in the *Bison*. Photographs and detailed, informative commentaries described the high points in most annual Greek shows and one spring probate show. The reviews contain information about terms for stepping and such types of steps as retrospects (celebrating a society's history and favorite steps); saluting (imitating other performances in a positive way); and cracking (making fun of another group). They also reveal typical costumes, props, and poses as well as the increased use of spectacle and cracking. Many shows offered cash prizes, which heightened competitiveness. Judging criteria typically includ-ed "showmanship, creativity, originality, precision, and crowd appeal." Stepping's increasing prominence is evident in the photographs chosen to represent each Greek-letter society in the pages profiling organizations. In the 1983 *Bison,* for example, Alpha Phi Alpha, Omega Psi Phi, and Phi Beta Sigma featured one photograph each of their respective step shows, and Phi Beta Sigma entitled their page "The Technicians of Step."[28]

The most prevalent term used for the Greek show performances in the 1980s was *stepping,* although synonyms occurred. "Steppin' Out," the *Bison*'s first Greek show commentary, for example, echoes a word employed earlier, re-ferring to the 1980 show as "a delightful demonstration of precision by the Greek organizations here on Howard's campus." And Robert Warren refers to steps as "marches" when he describes the Alpha Phi Alpha brothers "daz-zling the crowd with a crisp rendition of marches" in their 1981 show.[29]

The *Bison* captured steppers' frequently made assertion that stepping is not dancing. In the 1989 show, the Omegas declared "they were here for a step-show not a dance competition," and the brothers of Kappa Kappa Psi said they "didn't need music to step by."[30]

Retrospect routines help steppers celebrate their society's history and fa-vorite steps, and in 1980 Omega Psi Phi did so with "Omega in Retro-spect."[31] Each fraternity and sorority usually has at least one step recount-ing the key facts of their founding. Through associating their favorite steps with their founding story, they signal that these steps are worthy of praise and remembrance. Retrospects thus help to create traditional steps.

During the 1980s, groups used elaborate spectacles to generate crowd appeal. In the 1981 show, three fraternities "burst through paper and crepe hangings for their entrance marches," and the Deltas concealed an electric piano in "a giant silver pyramid." The Omegas "entered the gymnasium through the mouth of a huge wooden dog constructed in the shape of a doghouse." Members of Alpha Kappa Alpha (fig. 23) and Phi Beta Sigma burst through large banners or signs in the 1986 show, a popular way of creating drama and suspense. A photograph from the 1987 show depicts two Delta sisters standing in front of a large box that has a curtained doorway labeled "box of transformation." According to the caption, they entered the box as AKAs and emerged as Deltas.[32]

Steppers use contemporary hit tunes to capture audience attention, as Sherri Bowen reveals in "Showing Off" (1985). The Omegas entered the stage to the title tune from Prince's hit film *Purple Rain,* and the Zetas danced to Sheila

Figure 23. A popular way of creating spectacle and suspense in step shows involves bursting through banners, arches, or boxes. The caption noted, "Bursting through the front page of the 'AKA Times,' Malena Calvin and her sorors shredded the myth that AKA's are too pretty to step. The 'AKA Machine' proved that it was adept at imitating the men's steps." (1987 Howard University *Bison,* p. 43, courtesy of the Moorland-Spingarn Research Center, Howard University Archives)

E's "Glamorous Life."[33] Dressed in suits and heels and stepping to the tune "Phly Girls" in 1986, AKA claimed they were "born to be 'phly'" (fig. 24). Many captions reveal information about the popular costumes, props, and poses of the organizations. A photograph of a Kappa brother with his cane carries the caption "CANE TAPPING. As has become custom, the Kappas used canes in their performance." Alpha brothers in Egyptian headdresses stand,

Figure 24. Celebrating their ladylike image, AKA sorors display their "skee-wee" hand sign and are described as "so SUPREME." (1986 Howard University *Bison*, p. 62, courtesy of the Moorland-Spingarn Research Center, Howard University Archives)

their arms folded beneath their chins in a typical stepping pose (fig. 25). Creatively mixing nonverbal metaphors in the 1987 show, the Alphas combined Egyptian-looking costumes and headdresses with combat boots and war paint, signifying both their African heritage and the warlike nature of the competition (fig. 26). Again they stand and use the same arm pose, an arm position Phi Beta Sigma also adopted for the same show.[34]

Cracking on other fraternities and sororities played a major role during the 1980s. The 1986 Greek show's theme, "We Are One," seems calculated to counter the potentially divisive effects of cracking. Despite that theme, Sherri Milner observes, various groups cracked on their rivals anyway. Alpha Phi Omega, a service organization, "imitated moves" of Kappa Alpha Psi and Phi Beta Sigma and "mimicked the 'Q-dogs' of Omega Psi Phi and

Figure 25. The Alpha brothers. The caption reads "TO OUR ROOTS. The men of Alpha Phi Alpha emphasized the importance of African heritage." (1986 Howard University *Bison*, p. 62, courtesy of the Moorland-Spingarn Research Center, Howard University Archives)

Figure 26. The Alpha brothers. (1988 Howard University
Bison, p. 38, courtesy of the Moorland-Spingarn Research
Center, Howard University Archives)

their sometimes lewd and risqué movements." For their part of the performance, Alpha Phi Alpha—"First of all, servants to all, transcending all"—
promised the audience that they would be "proud and rocky, cold and
cocky." The Alphas "fascinated the audience with their ability to do a take
off on other fraternities." Portraying the Kappas as "conceited, self-centered,
egotistical men," two Alphas came out dressed in the Kappas' red and white
colors; "one wore a long fur coat and each admired the other as the audience rolled with laughter." Delta Sigma Theta "parodied the other sororities and made many crushing disregards to AKA, an apparent rival."[35]

The pose of haughty disdain visually demonstrates superiority over one's rivals. Deltas in the 1986 Greek show posed with their left hands on their hips, right arms held high in the air. As the caption reads, "Chins lifted haughtily, Delta Kelli Coleman and her sorors snapped their fingers in disdain of the ladies of AKA, and stepped their way to first place."[36] The Zetas, in turn, "dismiss[ed] their competitors to the amusement of the audience" by striking a nonverbal cracking pose in the 1987 show (fig. 27).

Intense cracking continued in the 1987 Greek show. As if recognizing that the only way to truly stand out was to deviate from the norm of cracking,

Figure 27. Members of Zeta Phi Beta sorority strike a cracking pose. (1988 Howard University *Bison*, p. 39, courtesy of the Moorland-Spingarn Research Center, Howard University Archives)

AKA sorority boldly stated, "When you've got it like this, there's no need to crack!" According to the *Hilltop*, "The AKA's surprised the audience by calling for unity among the greek-letter organizations" and "did not go the usual route of degrading other sororities." Yet AKA still gained audience approval through their tribute to Omega Psi Phi fraternity, doing "a sailor's salute as they approached the middle of the floor" and a "perfect imitation" of Omega moves that "brought the house down."[37]

Other organizations, however, continued to attract audience attention through cracks. The Zetas "left the audience rolling with laughter, as they showered disparaging comments on rival sororities." Phi Beta Sigma took "the members of Alpha Phi Alpha to 'stepping school.' They begged the Alphas to pay close attention while they performed a series of feet stomping, hand clapping, body rolling steps that won the audience's heart. When they finished, the stepmaster and President of Phi Beta Sigma, Jerrad Carter, declared, 'Class Dismissed!'" The Alphas' "'Don't Mess with My Steppin' Shoes' segment," in which they "parodied the other fraternities," attracted great attention. Alpha Phi Alpha "commented on the members of Omega Psi Phi Fraternity by inquiring about their GPA's [grade-point averages]. They portrayed the members of Kappa Alpha Psi as 'sweet boys' and ridiculed their use of canes when they step. Also, according to the Alphas, the Sigmas 'step like hillbillies right off the farm.'"[38]

One way of mocking rivals involves the skillful use of colors, costumes, props, and poses, as a 1982 Greek show commentary reveals: "The exquisite ladies of Delta Sigma Theta Sorority immediately proceeded to dazzle the crowd with an introduction of 'Yo Baby' in their red and white pants outfits resembling jump suits . . . with Pam Middleton at the lead with a pink and green cane. However, 'Yo Baby Yo' became 'No Baby No.' They then combined well-coordinated footwork with mixed sultry vocals to present a splendid show that aroused a grand applause from the audience."[39]

A first reading of this commentary suggests that the Deltas might have been saluting the Kappas by imitating their use of canes, but they might also have been cracking on the AKA sorority, whose colors are pink and green. "Yo Baby Yo" is widely known as a Kappa Alpha Psi signature or trade step, and Kappas are famous for their dexterous use of red and white striped canes. By carrying a pink and green cane, the colors of their archrivals, the group's leader may have been cracking on AKA. The word change, "No Baby No," suggests a playful crack, but the *Bison* does not contain the words of the performance.

A telephone interview with Pam Middleton in 1995 confirmed that the pink and green cane was a crack on the AKAs. But, Middleton explained, they were also cracking on the Kappas not saluting them and that the step caused controversy. The Deltas used the crack step to comment on a recent camaraderie that had developed between the Kappas and AKA. Because Middleton was a Kappa Sweetheart, she knew their steps well. She was able to borrow a Kappa cane, which she covered in pink and green. The other sorors carried pink and green handkerchiefs, which they held to their noses in a snobbish gesture, flicked twice in the air, and then dropped to the floor, mocking the prissy reputation of AKA, all to the words of "No Baby No." Middleton explained that the crack was carried out nonverbally through the colors, poses, and mocking use of "Yo Baby Yo." They did not add any new words other than changing "Yo" to "No." As Middleton observed, "Color is an easy way of knowing who you were going to mock."[40]

Deltas used similar color symbolism to crack on AKA in the 1985 show when they discarded pink and green AKA colors to step in Deltas' red and white (fig. 28). Because Deltas originally formed as a breakaway group from AKA, the initial camouflage in AKA colors followed by their removal and

Figure 28. "NUMBER ONE. After discarding their rival's colors, the Deltas stepped to place number one in the female category." (1986 Howard University *Bison*, p. 63, courtesy of the Moorland-Spingarn Research Center, Howard University Archives)

a proud display of Delta's true colors, works as a highly visual and readily understood barb.

The excitement generated by step shows sometimes leads to problems with crowd control. Even though the 1981 Greek show was noncompetitive, a lack of security allowed the "riotous crowd outside of Burr Gymnasium" to storm into the building, injuring three students in the process, Robert Warren notes. In response to cracking steps in the 1985 show, audience members displayed "flaring tempers and unruly behavior" in three "disorderly outbursts."[41]

One of the few descriptions of a different type of step show—the probate show—appears in the 1988 *Bison*. In "Probation prior to Vacation" Karen Samuels provides colorful details about the performances of five pledge clubs, demonstrating the importance of movement, song, and symbolic costumes:

> Shortly after noon, the five Pixie Kittens of the Archonian Pledge Club of Zeta Phi Beta Sorority Incorporated made their way through the waiting crowd to the space cleared away for their performance. These ladies, dressed in blue and white, each carried a stuffed white pixie kitten and had their hands turned down like paws, in imitation of their namesake. Relinquishing the kittens to their proud big sisters, they began their performance. Vowing love to Zeta and affirming that there was no doubt that they had made the right choice; these ladies stamped their feet, clapped their hands and sang of loyalty to their sorority.
>
> Immediately following the Pixie Kittens were the seven Dogs of the Crescent Pledge Club of Phi Beta Sigma Fraternity Incorporated. Wearing blue berets, blue combat boots and blue overalls; these men trod through the throng. The berets were removed, as were the overalls, to reveal white pants, suspenders, and blue shirts. In an exciting acrobatic display that involved variations on break dancing, these men wowed the crowd, as they claimed their superiority to other fraternities and bragged of their sexual prowess.

The caption of one of the four accompanying color photographs uses the word *grit* to describe a characteristic expression displayed by pledges—a stern face with an out-thrust lower lip (fig. 29). There are also photographs of the AKA pledge club; the Delta pledges performing their ritual duck walk (fig. 30); and the "Nubian Apes of Alpha Phi Alpha Fraternity, Inc.," who "let out whoops and snatched members of the audience into their arms as they prepare to cross the burning sands into Alpha land."[42]

Figure 29. "Face contorted in the familiar 'grit' of a
pledge, Conrad Thomas, a member of the Crescent, displays the struggle and determination required to endure
the pledge period and attain membership in a fraternity."
(1988 Howard University *Bison,* p. 14, courtesy of the
Moorland-Spingarn Research Center, Howard University
Archives)

Figure 30. "In a series of motions that have become a ritual in their Probate show program, the ducks of Delta Sigma Theta perform on the yard after their death march." Note the "get-down quality" prized in African dance as well as the symbolism of the lowly status of pledges. (1988 Howard University *Bison*, p. 15, courtesy of the Moorland-Spingarn Research Center, Howard University Archives)

The 1990s: "The Business of Steppin'"

During the first half of the 1990s a heightened sense of competitiveness and a preference for cash-award competitions characterized the annual Greek show. Stepping emerged as a money-making activity, both on and off campus, and steppers found new public arenas for their art.

In the 1990 show, the Zetas "dazzled the crowd with their salute to Greek Unity by imitating the various fraternities" and brought "the crowd to their feet once more with their blind-folded stepping." Emphasizing "Basic Hard Stepping, No Gimics!" the Phi Beta Sigma brothers asked the crowd to "watch them sweat." Angel Goldsborough recalls that "wild screams and applause could be heard throughout their whole performance." In addition to the Zetas' blindfolded stepping, the Alphas also "'stepped to a higher ground' while blindfolded," and Kappa Alpha Psi "awed the crowd when they swung their canes at high velocities while being blindfolded" in the 1992 show. These first references to blindfolds suggest a heightened, virtuoso attempt at showmanship, because stepping while blindfolded demands supreme unity and coordination.[43]

The Pan-Hellenic Council and the Howard University's Homecoming Steering Committee sponsored two homecoming step shows in 1991. Although the on-campus Pan-Hellenic show was noncompetitive, the larger, off-campus show had "cash prizes of $1200 going to the winners" and part of the revenue going to a local homeless shelter, Sonja Morris reported. In "The Business of Steppin'" Donna Lee highlights the commodification of stepping and quotes Andrew Johnstone, a member of Phi Beta Sigma: "Stepping should be taken seriously because it's a business and money is involved."[44]

Competition for prize money continued in 1992, with anticipation especially high. For the first time in many years all eight Greek-letter societies stepped in the show. Zeta Phi Beta's ability to salute all the historically black fraternities took them to first place, while judges disqualified Phi Beta Sigma for their "explicit lyrics."[45]

Steppers at Howard University began to find a wider audience for their talents in the early 1990s. Alpha Phi Alpha stepped in President Bill Clinton's Inaugural festivities after appearing in a commercial for Footlocker in December 1992. The Alphas expanded their audience further when the team traveled to South Africa in 1995. In workshops with children, the step team demonstrated their art and joined South Africans in gumboot dancing, which, some believe, may have influenced African American stepping.[46]

Taking cracking to the extreme by displaying guns onstage, AKA "shocked" the audience of the 1993 Greek show with an "unlady-like skit," wrote James Martin, and also pretended to execute "three so-called sororities." The Alphas cracked nonverbally on rivals in the same show: "They proceeded to mock the Kappas by stepping off-beat and dropping canes and the Omegas by crawling on the floor like dogs." The Alphas further mocked the Omegas by posing in an Omega stance, arms held up to form the shape of the letter Omega (fig. 31).[47]

The growing commercialization of the annual Greek show led people to question the effects of its commodification. To Shaunda Barrett, writing to the *Hilltop*'s editor, "Homecoming is now nothing more than a commercial fundraiser." Reacting to the off-campus locations of both the homecoming football game and the step show, Tushon Robinson pointed out that the old tradition of fraternities and sororities gathering around their respective plots on campus to enjoy reunion "would be worthless because no one will be there for them." Following the 1993 homecoming, the *Hilltop* editor observed that there was nothing wrong with the university making money on homecoming, but "why did it cost $12.50 to go to the Greek show?"[48]

Howard University hosted the first national championship step show during homecoming in 1994. The grand-prize winner received $2,500.

Figure 31. By appropriating an Omega stance, "Steven Powell, Donnie Hoskey, and the rest of the Alpha Phi Alpha step team mock the Omegas at the D.C. Armory." (1994 Howard University *Bison*, p. 28, courtesy of the Moorland-Spingarn Research Center, Howard University Archives)

"'More than one team will represent some of the organizations and teams outside of the Pan-Hellenic Council will step. . . . We are trying to broaden the show so people can see different kinds of stepping,' said Monique Woods, step show coordinator." The Pan-Hellenic Council, however, threatened to boycott the Homecoming Step Show over "the amount of prize money and the way funds have been distributed in past years."[49]

The Evolution of Stepping on College Campuses

The published record of stepping at Howard University confirms claims from around the United States that stepping evolved from the marching on line and group singing inherent in pledging rituals. Marching on line, the first ritual performance photographed, appeared in the 1943 and 1947 editions of the *Bison*. Although Van Taylor suggests that fraternities may have stepped at Howard as early as 1925, stepping evolved at different rates on other campuses. Kappa Alpha Psi member Thomas Harville, who pledged at West Virginia State College, recalls that in 1940 his fraternity participated in group singing, often while holding hands or moving in a circle, but they did not step. Another Kappa reported that his fraternity began stepping during the 1940s and developed it by marching on line while pledging: "Through the years brothers added singing and dancing, and in recent years we started using canes when we step." That corroborates the *Wall Street Journal*'s statement that stepping's "synchronized and syncopated moves date back to the 1940s, when lines of fraternity pledges marched in lockstep around campus in a rite of initiation." Julian Bond remembers stepping contests during his student days at Morehouse College in the late 1950s, note Freeman and Witcher. Anne Mitchum Davis, a Alpha Kappa Alpha who pledged at Lincoln University in Jefferson City, Missouri, noted that her sorority did not step during the 1950s but did more balletlike "synchronized dancing" than the "stomping kinds of things" men did. Fraternity alumni who worked at Virginia Tech in 1984 have recalled that blocking or stepping at their various colleges and universities in the 1950s involved singing, with only some movement and that usually in a circle. Robert J. Cummings, chair of the African studies department at Howard University and an alumnus of Florida A&M University, has said that in the early 1960s his fraternity, Omega Psi Phi, had stepped and used the term *stepping* as well as the terms *stomp* and *march*.[50]

Photographs from the Howard University yearbook suggest that during the 1960s counterclockwise circles were the most commonly photographed pattern of pledging rituals. Such movement is common in African dance and in African American juba and ring shouts. The photographs confirm statements about early stepping often being part of a singing event, mainly in a circle.

The first picture of an indoor stepping event before a large audience— and the first reference to a formalized pledge group program called "Greek Weekend"—occurred in the 1965 *Bison*. Terms for stepping change over time and vary among campuses across the United States. At Howard University, the word *demonstrate* was first used in the 1964 *Hilltop* and in the

1969 *Bison* to describe stepping. "Demonstration" appears repeatedly and prominently for stepping during the 1970s until 1976, after which it no longer appears except as a faint echo in the 1981 *Bison*. Yet none of the informants from Howard whom I interviewed in 1995 used the term *demonstration*, and none had heard of its use. Other synonyms for stepping, such as "bop," "stomping," and "marches," appeared in the campus newspaper and yearbook in the 1960s and 1970s. During the 1980s and 1990s, informants at Virginia Tech used the terms *stepping* and *blocking*, and students at California State, Fullerton used the term *marching* during the 1980s, no doubt reflecting the influence of black drill teams and marching bands as well as marching on line.[51]

The photographic record over the years shows the continuity of nonverbal codes, costumes, and icons. The 1965 *Bison*, for example, pictures a common arm movement that was still seen in 1995 (fig. 11). Shaved heads, a look that remains popular among male probates (as well as among many African American men), appear in photographs in the 1963 and 1967 *Bison* among Kappas and Omegas. Pictures of 1995 Omega probates reveal appearances similar to their 1967 counterparts (figs. 13, 14). Alpha Phi Alpha used Egyptian garb as far back as 1943 to symbolize their African identity, and Omega Psi Phi appears in dog collars and leashes and gathered around the Dial on the Howard University campus, where they still perform. Despite a reaffirmation of an official ban on canine imagery by the national Omega Psi Phi office in 1984, Howard probates still affected canine barks and growls in 1995 as brothers taunted them with bones. Combat boots and war paint symbolize the intense competition between rival groups, and photographs capture the traditional stoic facial expressions of probates, which are referred to in the *Bison* as the "grit" (fig. 29).

By the 1981 edition of the *Bison*, stepping had come into its own as a tradition deserving of detailed performance reviews that reveal the importance of spectacle, popular music, and virtuoso performances, such as stepping while blindfolded. The first reference to stepping while blindfolded appeared in the 1991 *Bison* and in several shows thereafter.

Audiences respond enthusiastically to stepping, and emotions sometimes run high. The 1981 and 1982 yearbooks describe large and boisterous crowds. Rowdy outbursts and flaring tempers among the audience temporarily halted the 1985 show, which featured many cracking steps. Numerous examples of both cracking and saluting appear in *Bison* commentaries and photographs. Cracking on rival groups, prominent in the 1980s and early 1990s, became extreme in 1993, when the AKAs carried guns onstage.

During the 1990s stepping became increasingly popular and commodified.

It was featured in commercial advertisements; the first syndicated television show of an annual national stepping competition, *S.T.O.M.P.* (*Step Out National Championships*), appeared; and prize money for winning step teams grew. While Alpha Phi Alpha at Howard University traveled to South Africa, exporting their stepping traditions, numerous fraternity and sorority members across the country shared their stepping talents with churches, schools, and community groups (chapter 4).

Researching the written record of stepping in black Greek-letter organizations could be repeated at other colleges and universities in order to provide a comparative look at the emergence of this tradition. Despite stepping's nature as an ephemeral dance form, the amount of journalistic coverage it has attracted at Howard University suggests that stepping has played a significant role in student life. It also plays a vital role in the rite of passage to brotherhood and sisterhood.

2 / A Ritual Dance of Identity

We are the brothers of Que Psi Phi,
the Mother Pearl and that's no lie.
We're gonna live, we're gonna die
in the name of Que Psi Phi.
—Omega Psi Phi Fraternity, Inc., probate show,
    Howard University, spring 1995

With shaven heads and gold paint glistening on their faces, the 1995 probates of Omega Psi Phi at Howard University stand at rigid attention, holding across their chests shields decorated with the fraternity insignia (fig. 14).
In combat boots, tan trousers, blue sweatshirts, and sunglasses, the young
men stand with their chins and lower lips thrust out, a ritual facial expression known as "the grit." A large crowd of Omega brothers, friends, and
students mills noisily around. Despite taunts from the crowd, the probates
stand unmoving, preserving their cool demeanor. Suddenly, the step leader
sings out, "No blood." The others respond, "No blood, no sweat. We're
the brothers of love, pledging Que Psi Phi." Breaking into a vigorous step,
the brothers sing about their decision to become Omegas. Following that
physically taxing number, they break into a mournful tune (fig. 32). They
sing as they stand tall, holding their shields underneath their chins, of how
pledging has changed their lives:

> *Refrain: Leader:* Oh Oh Oh!
> *All:* Oh Oh Oh!
> *Leader:* Oh Oh Oh Oh!
> *All:* Oh Oh Oh Oh!
> *Leader:* We are the brothers of Que Psi Phi,
> *All:* We are the brothers of Que Psi Phi,
> *Leader:* the Mother Pearl and that's no lie.
> *All:* the Mother Pearl and that's no lie.

Leader: We're gonna live, we're gonna die
All: We're gonna live, we're gonna die
Leader: in the name of Que Psi Phi.
All: in the name of Que Psi Phi.
Leader: We've come from near we've come from far
All: We've come from near we've come from far
Leader: first by lamp and then by star.
All: first by lamp and then by star.

Refrain

Leader: In this place of pain and tears,
All: In this place of pain and tears,
Leader: I have learned to persevere.
All: I have learned to persevere.
Leader: Manhood and scholarship,
All: Manhood and scholarship,
Leader: and the meaning of uplift.
All: and the meaning of uplift.
Leader: Cooper, Coleman, Love, and Just (*varied rhythm*),
All: Cooper, Coleman, Love, and Just,
Leader: They are watching over us.
All: They are watching over us.

Refrain

Leader: I may not see my home again,
All: I'll wave good-bye to all my friends,
Leader: I'll tell my Mama not to cry,
All: I am pledging Que Psi Phi.

Refrain

Leader: She said, "Son along the way,
All: She said, "Son along the way,
Leader: watch those cloudy skies of gray.
All: watch those cloudy skies of gray.
Leader: The sun is on the other side } (*ritardando*)
All: the sun is on the other side, }
Leader: shining brightly Que Psi Phi." }
All: shining brightly Que Psi Phi." } (*crescendo*)

Refrain (resume previous tempo)

The probates slowly make their way across the Yard to the Omega plot
near Thirkield Hall, where the fraternity was founded. There, they kneel

Figure 32. "We Are the Brothers of Que Psi Phi" as sung by Omega Psi Phi fraternity, Howard University, 1995.

around the granite monument dedicated in 1975 to the memory of the four founders: Oscar J. Cooper, Frank Coleman, Edgar A. Love, and Ernest E. Just. All the other Omega brothers gather in a circle surrounding the probates. Arms locked together and swaying slowly from side to side, they sing the Omega hymn. Encircling the probates, the fraternity publicly acknowledges its new brothers.[1]

Although the show took place several years after the pledging process was eliminated by the NPHC, probate shows at Howard University remain highly visible public rites of passage as young men and women celebrate their new brotherhood and sisterhood. Tradition is evident among Omega probates, who sport the same look as their counterparts did in 1967 (figs. 13, 14). In a probate show, stepping most forcefully reveals its nature as an aesthetic ritual of group identity tied to the social drama of pledging a Greek-letter society.

For many college students, being accepted by one of the nine organizations in the NPHC constitutes a transformative experience that will influence their entire lives. Not only will they gain access to a powerful network of leaders within their own fraternity or sorority, but they will also build associations with those in other Greek-letter societies. Ozell Sutton, a former president of Alpha Phi Alpha's national organization, maintains that active members of black fraternities and sororities "are the best trained, most highly experienced, and most influential people in the black community." Black Greeks constitute a "network that cannot be matched anywhere in the black community. The NAACP can't match it; it doesn't have the highly trained and sophisticated people you'll find in a fraternity or sorority. Even the black church doesn't have it." For those committed to ideals of social justice, uplift, service, and scholarship, the black Greek network provides members with "social capital." A brother or sister who needs help to further a cause can find support through this network.[2]

Even a brief look at the projects that black Greek-letter societies support attests to the greater strength that comes through numbers. In 1981, for example, Omega Psi Phi fraternity endowed its first Omega Faculty Chair at Rust College in Holly Springs, Mississippi. During the 1980s, Omega Psi Phi also completed its $250,000 contribution to the United Negro College Fund and pledged an annual gift of $50,000 to that organization in perpetuity. So strong are these social networks that one white student at Virginia Tech told me that he had chosen to pledge a black Greek-letter society. Not only did the stepping attract him, but he also thought the social networking the fraternity provided would be better than that granted by white fraternities. The student became president as well as stepmaster of the Alpha Phi Alpha chapter at Virginia Tech.[3]

Johnny Ford, the first African American mayor of Tuskegee, Alabama, who pledged Kappa Psi Phi fraternity at Knoxville College in 1962, attests to the value of the brotherhood he developed through his fraternity: "The college fraternity was a good experience for me. As a matter of fact, when I left college, went to New York, couldn't find a job, was about to starve, was out of money, about to be put out of the YMCA, my Kappa brother and I thought, let's call the Kappa House. And I called the Kappa House and they took us in, under their wings, and gave us a place to stay and helped me find a job."[4]

Members of alumni chapters sometimes continue to step and participate in intercollegiate step teams that compete in a growing number of stepping competitions. In 1999 such teams as the D.C. Coalition of Alpha Phi Alpha, Inc. (eight graduates from the years 1986 to 1997) and the All Stars of Iota Phi Theta (eight graduates from the years 1992 through 1997) have participated in the Philly Greek Stepshow. Dwayne Dixon, acting executive director of Iota Phi Theta, recalls how he and other members of the graduate chapter of his fraternity in Chicago competed in the national stepping competition at the 1995 Iota Conclave:

> In 1995, in St. Louis, my alumni chapter here in Chicago decided that we would do something unusual for a graduate chapter and participate in the National Step Competition. There had been much good-natured grumbling among the older heads in the fraternity that the younger members had lost touch with some of the traditional elements of stepping as practiced by Iota Phi Theta. We figured we old dogs could teach the young fellas a few new tricks.
>
> The conclave was to take place in July of 1995, so starting in March of 1995 we began practicing every Saturday. We started in the driveway of one of the team members. As the practices became more involved, we moved to my patio and eventually to the basketball court in my subdivision.
>
> What you have to remember is that we are talking about a group of older guys here—the youngest of us was thirty and I was thirty-four at the time. These are much older bones at work, but we took it very seriously! We went as far as to sit at an electric piano and record background music for a couple of traditional fraternity songs to be included in the performance.
>
> After many aches and pains (and no small amount of laughter and abuse from our spouses) we performed in the National Step Competition at Conclave. And in what I suppose is the ultimate proof that "virtue is its own reward" we took first prize in the show![5]

Stepping is sometimes performed at the weddings and funerals of members. Thus, not only does it function as one ritual in joining a black Greek organization, but it also continues as well in other important rites of passage.

Rite of Passage to Brotherhood and Sisterhood

In his classic work *The Rites of Passage,* Arnold van Gennep writes, "The life of an individual in any society is a series of passages from one age to another and from one occupation to another." Expanding on van Gennep's ideas, Victor Turner argues that these passage rites mark transitions from social invisibility to visibility (as in birth and puberty rites) and social visibility to social invisibility (as in funeral rites) as well as a sociosexual conjunction (as in marriage rites). Joining an African American Greek-letter society involves a transition to greater social visibility as well as a fictive kinship of brotherhood or sisterhood.[6]

The rituals involved with joining a fraternity or sorority include the same three phases that van Gennep and Turner identify as part of the ritual process. The first phase is separation from the initiate's previous life. The second is a transition period called liminality, which Turner defines as "a betwixt-and-between condition often involving seclusion from the everyday scene." The third and final stage is reaggregation or reincorporation into the everyday world.[7]

Because many fraternity and sorority rituals are secret, it is impossible to write about all of the rituals employed in joining such a group. Some, however, such as "going on line," from which stepping may have developed, and probate step shows, are visible to the larger community. They mark stages in the incorporation of new members into a social brotherhood or sisterhood. Even step shows that are not part of the ritual of incorporating new members may be viewed as rituals that create, maintain, and celebrate group identity.

In 1990 the Presidents Council of the NPHC took a strong stance against hazing by voting to replace pledging with an intake process in which new members are chosen on the basis of a written application, and their respective memberships ratified their decision. New members participate in a two-week intake process in which they learn the history and values of their new Greek-letter society. Some inducted under the old pledging process refer to themselves as "old school" and the post–1990 members as "new school."

The terms *old school* and *new school* appear as early as 1975 in the Howard campus newspaper. In response to a front-page article by Michael A. Cressey that criticized the Beta chapter of Alpha Phi Alpha for alleged hazing, Steven R. Jones pegs Cressey's arguments as "indicative of the 'Old School' vs. the 'New School' ideologies of pledging." He continues, "The 'Old School' concept of pledging invariably involved the use of physical and mental duress as ways and means of accomplishing the objectives of the pledge period, whereas the 'new school' involves essentially coming and signing on the dotted line to become a member of a Greek letter fraternity or sorority." Jones defends the "old school" pledging process by arguing that "one will not appreciate something which he is striving towards if there is no sacrifice or toil. I dare not say that I would care as much about my Fraternity and my Fraternity brothers if all I had to do was come and sign up for membership." Jones argues that if the "new school" is "allowed to completely prevail as the method of pledging, then this will undoubtedly be the 'death of the Black fraternities and sororities.'"[8]

Jones's sentiments are still alive. Some old school members may refer to new school members when they are not present in terms that indicate they did not have to work as hard to join the organization. As Tina Harris notes, the terms *paper* (automatically becoming a member by signing a piece of paper), *skaters* ("not working hard to get into the organization—skating in"), or *t-shirt-wearers* express some of the "negative feelings and animosity" that have surfaced as a result of the changes in the way members are selected.[9]

In recalling the stages he went through to join Kappa Alpha Psi at Knoxville College in 1962, Johnny Ford reveals that the process lasted at least six months. It began when he joined an organization called the TIKs ("Temporary Inclined Kappas"). After attending a "smoker," an informational session about the fraternity, Ford was selected into the pledge club ("the Scrollers") in the spring: "And during the summer time is when you would practice. For example, I remember working in New Jersey and we would practice all summer on our steps, and big brothers would work with us and then when we came back in the fall, we were on line, and you have a week of pledging. That whole week you were moved out of the dorm and moved out in the gymnasium. They would harass you and you would have to do all kinds of crazy things. . . . Do things for the big brothers."[10]

Once on line, Ford recalls, "You'd come out of the cafeteria, and everyone would be waiting for the Kappas and the Ques and the Alphas and the Sigmas and the AKAs and the Deltas." As part of parading and marching on line, Ford remembers performing the following step with his cane, a trademark of Kappa Alpha Psi, which cultivates the image of being debonair gentlemen. The words are sung, and (x) represents a missing downbeat:

Here comes Kappa down the walk,
everybody's talking 'bout the way they walk.
Carrying their canes by their side,
reaching in the sky for Phi Nu Pi.

With a long and a short and a
(x) long short
and a long and a short and a
(x) long short
and a hup! two, three, four
hup! two, three, four.[11]

Under the intake process, the old ritual of going on line has been eliminated. The predominant public ritual associated with the passage to brotherhood or sisterhood is now stepping. Within the many movements, chants,
and songs of stepping, one can glimpse elements of the ritual process that
have been suppressed from other public venues. For example, although the
practice of pledges going on line and marching around campus together and
dressed alike is no longer allowed, new pledges frequently march on line as
part of a step show. Thus, the artistic venue of a step show permits rituals
to be performed that are no longer sanctioned in other contexts.

The words members use to refer to themselves, each other, and the stages of their incorporation into the societies shed light on the general ritual
process of joining such a group. My discussion of this process includes both
the pre–1990 era of pledging, which I will refer to as the "old process," and
the post–1990 era of the intake process. In some cases, terms from the pledging era are still used even though the behavior to which that the term refers
has been extremely modified or, in some cases, has disappeared. "Line," a
commonly heard word from the pledging era, for example, referred to persons who were pledging or had pledged together, Kimbrough reports. Undergraduates initiated together through the intake process still refer to themselves as "a line," even though they are not supposed to enact the old ritual
of marching on line. In the old process, which would last about six weeks,
line sisters or brothers would be arranged by height. They would use terms
such as "my front" or "my back" for members in front of or behind them
and would refer to fellow pledges by their line number. "Number One"
referred to the shortest member, and higher numbers referred to taller members. Members who have pledged on the same line are sometimes called
"sans" or "sands," a term, Harris notes, that sometimes also refers to those
from other chapters who have pledged at the same time. Those who have
passed all aspects of the pledging or intake process are sometimes said to
have "crossed the sands" or to have "gone over," Kimbrough observes. The
phrase *go over* is an echo of the slavery period, when the term *going over*
in spirituals might refer not only to crossing the Jordan River to freedom
but also to crossing the Mason-Dixon line. The term *spesh* or *special* may

refer to the big sister assigned to protect the pledge (under the old process), and, Harris reports, may be used interchangeably between the big sister and her pledgee.[12]

Variant terms for persons who pledge together, such as "ship" and "shippee," allude to the shipping of slaves to America. Just as they were packed together in the crowded holds of ships, initiates often stand close together in a line. The first person in line is called the captain and the last person the anchor. "Ship" and "shippee" are used in parts of the Midwest, for example, in Illinois, Iowa, Michigan, and Kansas, Kimbrough notes.[13]

Just as verbal labels help define a ritual status that separates pledges from others, so do the nonverbal behaviors they adopt. As a sign of separation from their previous, non-Greek existence, pledges begin to adopt the traditional style of the organization they are pledging. Their jackets or t-shirts may bear the colors, nicknames, line numbers, and Greek letters of the society they hope to pledge. Harris observes that new school members are more likely to wear clothes "that communicate their membership to others." Some members call identifying clothes and artifacts "'nalia" (paraphernalia).[14] They may all wear similar hairstyles and greet each other with traditional hand signs or calls. Perhaps the most striking nonverbal facial expression that reveals the lowly, liminal status of pledges is what students throughout the country refer to as "the grit."

Appearing to grit their teeth, pledges performing in their first step show, called a "probate" or "neophyte" show, frequently affect a stoic demeanor as they stand in line with fellow pledges, their lower lips often thrust out (fig. 29). While they are questioned, examined, and sometimes taunted or criticized by members of the society they want to join, they strive to keep their cool and show respect by staring straight ahead without moving or showing emotion. The stance closely resembles that required by the military when new recruits stand stiffly at attention under review by their superiors. It is possible that returning black G.I.'s brought the grit to campuses when they joined fraternities after World War II and the Korean War. The compulsory ROTC participation required at Howard and other land-grant universities may also have contributed a military influence to stepping. According to a student from Brandeis University who visited Howard University in 1965, "A two-year, two-hour-a-week compulsory ROTC program for all male undergrads also typifies the administration's orientation. While it is true that every land grant school must have an ROTC program, Howard's requirement exceeds the federal requirement."[15]

In addition to ROTC and the influence of returned service men and women, military influences were perhaps from a tradition of the mock military reviews that developed among slaves. During "Training Day" performances, slaves "lampooned white military practices." Burlesque military-style parades flourished in the 1830s from New England to Georgia and later became a standard feature of minstrel shows and other forms of entertainment. Many African American benevolent and secret mutual aid societies enjoyed elaborate public parades and encouraged youths to participate in drill teams. Describing the various community drill team competitions in Philadelphia, Jerrilyn M. McGregory notes, "As in the military, an inspection initiates the drill." Most of the marchers are female and "assume bellicose facial expressions while in military formation." Because of their emphasis on piety and respectability, the black schools established by northern missionaries after the Civil War refused to allow students to dance. Some, however, "permitt[ed] them to 'march' on social occasions," E. Franklin Frazier notes.[16]

The grit also embodies the facial serenity prevalent in African sculpture and dance. Noting that many observers have commented on this facial composure, Robert Farris Thompson calls it the "mask of the cool." Thompson links the facial pose with deeply held African beliefs that coolness is "an all-embracing, positive attribute which combines notions of composure, silence, vitality, healing, and social purification."[17]

An indication of what the word *grit* might symbolize to those who assume that expression may be found in a poem written by Ruby Berkely Goodwin of Sigma Gamma Rho:

SIGMA SIGMA

It takes a little courage,
And a little self-control
And a grim determination
If you want to reach the goal.

It takes a deal of striving
And a firm and stern set chin
No matter what's the battle,
If you really want to win.

. . .

But its prizes call for fighting
For endurance and for grit
For a rugged disposition
And a don't know when to quit.[18]

Goodwin's poem is similar in content to "three traditional poems of the fraternal movement": "If" by Rudyard Kipling, "Invictus" by William E. Henley, and the anonymous "Don't Quit."[18]

During the pledging process, aspiring members affect many of the characteristics of liminality that Turner has found in his study of ritual among the Ndembu tribe in Africa as well as ritual in other parts of the world. A dominant feature of liminality is humility. The neophytes appear as a "tabula rasa, a blank slate, on which is inscribed the knowledge and wisdom of the group, in those respects that pertain to the new status." Through such ritual actions as dressing alike, being referred to by their line numbers, shaving their heads (in fraternities), and addressing big brothers or big sisters with deference and respect, pledges accept a lowly role that tests their commitment to their new brotherhood or sisterhood. Perhaps the earliest record of such liminal behavior among pledges at Howard is found in Van Taylor's 1925 account of the Omega Psi Phi pledges who "thrust their manly but unshaven chins high in the air on one day, and the very next bow their heads in meek submission, and bark even as the lowest canine in the street, at the demand of one who has experienced all the pangs of humiliation thru which he is just passing."[19]

At the same time that aspiring members are in a liminal state and separated from their former roles, they also experience the most powerful emotion of the ritual process. Turner calls this emotion "communitas," which he defines as a strong feeling of community or "communion of equal individuals who submit together to the general authority of the ritual elders." In the final stage of a probate step show, older members may express communitas with new pledges by joining them in the final step routine of the show, or encircling them in a kind of group embrace that symbolizes their incorporation into the society. The experience of such communitas is unforgettable. Recalling his own pledging experience with Omega Psi Phi in 1962 at Florida A&M University, Robert J. Cummings says, "I tell you the only thing that I can even think that is closest to it, at least when I went over, is a religious experience. Because the brothers and the whole community were caught up in it and there is this kind of egging you on, you know, inspiring you, challenging you, to be your very best self and to revere the good that is yours to share."[20]

In a larger sense, however, all Greek step shows both create and express communitas. The very act of performing such highly synchronized, intricate movements demands a profound communion of both spirit and body among all steppers. Anthropologist Edward Hall argues that people who live in close physical contact, such as families, gradually entrain their body rhythms to each other. The disciplined practice of stepping may help create the same type of entrainment, as the sharing of common movement and rhythmic patterns bonds steppers to each other. In order for a group to move and act as one, participants must subordinate individual movement patterns to the choreographed movement of the group. Frequently, as steppers and audience members mingle and greet each other at the end of a step show, an unstructured, "spontaneous communitas" occurs in the celebratory affirmation of group identity.[21]

Stepping and the Social Drama

In his poem "Among School Children," W. B. Yeats asks, "O body swayed to music, O brightening glance, / How can we know the dancer from the dance?"[22] Stepping helps both the dancers and the audience know more about the identities of individuals and the social groups with which they affiliate. It creates, perpetuates, and comments on the worldviews of participants and embodies the social drama from which worldviews arise.

Just as humans are sapient, tool-making, and symbol-using beings, so, too, are they performing beings maintains Victor Turner. But in calling humans "performers" ("homo performans"), Turner means much more than that they are entertainers. Rather, he says that humans are "self-performing animals." Their performances are reflexive; they reveal themselves to themselves. From performances, we gain both self-knowledge and knowledge about the larger society. "The actor may come to know himself better through acting or enactment," Turner observes, "or one set of human beings may come to know themselves better through observing and/or participating in performances generated and presented by another set of human beings."[23]

Building on sociologist Erving Goffman's ideas about the performance of self in everyday life, Turner bases his analyses of ritual on understanding the social dramas that give rise to them. By "social drama," Turner means a unit of "aharmonic or disharmonic social process, arising in conflict situations." Social dramas typically contain four phases of public action: a breach of regular social relations; a crisis in which the breach tends to widen; redressive action that "furnishes a distanced replication and critique of the events leading up to and composing the crisis"; and reintegration "of the disturbed social group or the social recognition and legitimation of irreparable schism between the contesting parties."[24]

The central social drama of fraternal organizations involves group maintenance. Each year some members graduate, and if they are not replaced by new members the social group will eventually die. Each year brings a breach created by the loss of old members and the opening for potential new members. During the pledging process (under the old system) or the intake process (under the new one) the crisis widens. Although potential members are trying to pledge or join the organization, they must be tested and found worthy by the membership. Various redressive actions attempt to resolve the crisis. By wearing the Greek paraphernalia of the society, for example, aspiring members attempt to look the part. By striving to learn the group's history, traditional calls, handshakes, and steps, they attempt to perform their sought-for new identity. By publicly performing in a step show with their line, the aspiring members metaphorically assert, through their performances, that they have become brothers or sisters. In reintegration, the final phase of the social drama of maintaining group membership, old members symbolically embrace new members publicly through such means as applauding, encircling, or stepping with them in a finale.

Within the social life of fraternal organizations, step shows function as highly visible redressive actions stimulated by the yearly breach and crisis caused by graduation of old members and the need to incorporate new ones. Because other groups also experience similar crises of new membership, competition is strong. Step shows provide a way to attract new members through a persuasive rhetoric of style and identity. In the "Founders Step," for example, Sigma Gamma Rho sisters at Virginia Tech not only repeat the facts about their sorority's origination, but they also attempt to define themselves as different from any other sorority in a step dedicated to one of their sorors:

> Seven women
> in 1922
> got together at Butler U.
> They set out on a mission
> seven decades ago
> to establish this sorority
> Sigma Gamma Rho!
> We come unique
> not like the rest
> the ladies of Sigma
> are nothing but the best.
> Besides gold,
> the color is blue,
> we dedicate this step to Mary Lou.

As members articulate their own group character through movements and words they also reflect on the character of competing societies. Steppers can either "salute" other groups by respectfully imitating their style (also known as "tribute" or "dedication" steps) or humorously mock them, which is known as "cracking," "dissing," or "cutting." Stepping performances are a key venue for displaying and asserting group identity as well as for negotiating the status of each group within the social order. According to Carol D. Branch, "The organization with the flashiest steps or the 'coolest' outfit at the step show tends to garner the most interest in terms of prospective members, thus aiding in the continuation of the various fraternities."[25]

As stepping evolved, many of the nine Greek-letter societies developed distinctive and characteristic steps and chants known as "trade" or "signature" steps that embody the ethos or character of a group and are nationally known by all its chapters. A few of the better-known trade steps are Alpha Phi Alpha's "Grand-daddy" and "Ice, Ice"; Alpha Kappa Alpha's "It's a Serious Matter"; Zeta Phi Beta's "Sweat" and "Precise"; Phi Beta Sigma's "Wood," "Sweat," and "Precision"; and Iota Phi Theta's "Centaur Walk" and "The Chick-a-Chow." Audiences instantly recognize them as "belonging" to a particular group. Different societies may refer to rivals in either a salutory or derogatory way by how they imitate these trade steps.

Members of Iota Phi Theta, the newest fraternity to be admitted to the NPHC, still recall the name of the person who invented their "Centaur Walk" and the year he did so. According to Dwayne Dixon, the "Centaur Walk" was invented in 1966 by Brother Robert Young at Morgan State University in Baltimore. Because the Centaur, after the shield, is one of Iota's "most readily identifying symbol," embodying that symbol through stepping is important. The Iota Web-page carries the information that the Centaur, a "mythical beast with the head and torso of a man, and the body of a stallion," is "near and dear to all Men of Iota Phi Theta. The mythology, characteristics, and legacy of The Centaur are a binding force within the Brotherhood." The Iota shield displays the image of a centaur, about to release an arrow from a bow. To evoke that image, the brothers mime pulling on a bow and arrow while they typically step three times to the left and three times to the right.[26]

Learning the "Centaur Walk" is part of the process of becoming an Iota Phi Theta brother, Dixon observes. "I mean if you've never been in a fraternity before, who's going to teach you how to step? Other brothers. And it's part of what they teach you. In addition to learning the requisite history and information about the fraternity, the 'Centaur Walk' is something that you must know." So important is this signature step to Iota Phi Theta that, Dixon recalls, "as long as I've been a brother, . . . , I think I may have seen one or two step shows in my whole life done by the fraternity where the 'Centaur Walk' was not done, and it was commented on. You will hear the commentary from the brothers in attendance. . . . It's like, 'Hey—where was the 'Centaur Walk?'"[27]

Even though trade steps are traditional, they change over time. When I asked Dixon to provide a few verses of the "Centaur Walk" chant, he said that it involves a call-and-response piece ("My brothers, what do you want?") and functions "like a framework, for other little mini-steps or breaks inside of it." Although "it has evolved," it is "a traditional step":

> I say, My bro-thers . . .
> —Yeah?
> I say, Who's fly?
> —I Phi!
> I say my . . . Iota-Phi brothers . . .
> —What do you want my brother?
> I say we're going to do . . .
> —What are we going to do?
> I say the Norfolk Slide!
> —He said the Norfolk Slide!

> At this point the "Norfolk Slide," which is a kind of "break," is executed. These breaks are usually four or eight bars long, and at the completion of the break the "Centaur Walk" resumes. Other examples of these breaks are "The Old-Time Sound," "The Scramble," "The Lookabout," "The Replace," and on and on. That's one of the nice things about the "Centaur Walk." Because of this structure, the basic framework retains the traditional aspect of the step and provides the link to the past. On the other hand, the breaks allow for creativity and keeping the step fresh and up to date.[28]

In addition to trade or signature steps, steppers use two other types of steps, saluting and cracking. These steps imitate two major poles or tensions within the complex social drama of black Greek life. The first is a tendency toward identification and unity with all black Greeks. Each of the nine NPHC member organizations have similar values and goals. Further, some fraternities and sororities tend to date members from other groups, and all Greek-letter societies share common experiences. Saluting another group by imitating their steps or style embodies this friendly impulse toward unity. For example, the sweetheart organization of Phi Beta Sigma, the Sigma Doves, saluted Phi Beta Sigma at the 1985 Blue and White Weekend Show at the University of Florida:

> I was walking down the street the other night,
> when I saw a fine guy dressed in blue and white.
> As he came my way I heard him say
> that Phi Beta Sigma is the only way.
> I say I like the Sigma Dove,
> so blue and white.[29]

The second pole or tension within the social drama of Greek life is a tendency toward competition and difference, because organizations compete for membership. The act of cracking, or making fun of another group, dramatizes the competition. A well-executed crack simultaneously elevates the status of the performers and lowers the status of the target group.

Like many Greek-letter societies, black fraternities and sororities are intensely competitive. The competitive spirit comes to the fore in the "crack" or cut whereby one group makes fun of another. Playful competition "stands at the center of the black aesthetic," Roger Abrahams notes. The movement play of African American children is full of mocking social commentary, Lee Ellen Friedland has observed, and Michael J. Bell reports that cracking plays an important role in the middle-class play of African American adults as well. The strong African American tradition of verbal dueling, expressed in such well-known folklore genres as the dozens ("snapping" or "sounding"), a verbal dueling game in which one person knocks another's mother, or rapping, signifying, and marking, influences the structure of many cracks. Steppers can also crack nonverbally by parodying the steps or style of another group. They often call nonverbal cracks "mocking" and "breaking it down."[30]

When Alpha Phi Alpha cracked on the Kappas outside a student dining hall at Virginia Tech in the spring of 1983, they used a popular cracking theme, "We're Laughing at You (figs. 33–35)." The step employs the folk tradition of signifying, which criticizes through indirection and innuendo. It also uses marking or mocking to make fun of the Kappas. One student stepped forward from the group and said:

I once (*points index finger*)
knew some Kappas
that went to this school.
They were sloooow walking (*exaggerated slow walk, as in slow motion*),
sweeeeet talking (*rubs hand over his hair*),
oh, oh,
so very, very cool (*closes eye and clinches fists in front of chest on the word cool*).

As if to underscore the message, another brother bent double in an exaggerated belly laugh—"ho-ho-ho." The success of this crack depends not only on the audience knowing that Kappa Alpha Psi cultivates a cool, playboy image but also on the performer's ability to imitate this style in a comic way. The cracking continued with the popular refrain used by fraternities and sororities alike: "I say we're laughing at you and you don't know why." The second line of the refrain rhymes with the first, and in this case the Alpha Phi Alpha brothers chant, "I say we're laughing at you cause you ain't A Phi!"[31]

Figures 33 and 34. At Virginia Tech, an Alpha Phi Alpha brother cracks on the Kappas' suave, sweet-talking image through "marking," a nonverbal imitation. In these two frames from a video, the performer is saying "sweeeeet talking." (1983, photograph and video by Hazen Robert Walker)

Figure 35. The cracking continues as the brother, using exaggerated facial and hand gestures, says, "so very, very cool." (1983, photograph and video by Hazen Robert Walker)

The Alphas use marking for "Your Mama Didn't Tell You 'bout A Phi A?" another cracking step that echoes the dozens, as in "your mama so ugly that when she cry, the tears run down her back." In the following step, performed outside a Virginia Tech dining hall in the spring of 1983 (fig. 36), Alpha Phi Alpha members crack on the style of the Sigmas (Phi Beta Sigma fraternity) and salute their own step by first performing it in an uncoordinated fashion (the way the Sigmas step). Then they perform it with the hard-stepping vigor that is a nationally recognized hallmark of Alpha Phi Alpha. One brother goes to the audience and brings a white woman student (a friend) to the center of the performing area. When the others form a large circle around her, he asks:

Brother: Who was the first person to tell you about A Phi A?

(*The woman smiles, shakes her head, and holds up her palms, empty-hand-ed, as if to say, "I don't know."*)

Brother: You mean to tell me, your

All: mama didn't tell you 'bout A Phi A?
  She didn't tell you 'bout the brothers and their sexy ways?
  She didn't tell you how they slide to the side so sweet?

(The group performs the verse with faint voices and uncoordinated, weak movements while they circle the woman.)

Stepmaster, interrupting verse: Hold on, stop, stop.

Brother: What's wrong, man?

Stepmaster: Cats, if we're gonna do this step,
   we can't look like a bunch of Sigmas.
   If you're gonna do this step,
   you have to put your heart in it, like this:

(loudly) **I said, Your**

All: **mama didn't tell you 'bout A Phi A.**
   She didn't tell you 'bout the brothers and their sexy ways.
   She didn't tell you how they slide to the side so sweet.
   She didn't tell you 'bout the first of all black Greeks.
   She didn't put you on her knee and break it on down.
   Uh! Uh! Uh! Uh! A Phi A!

(The group performs this verse loudly while skipping in a counterclockwise circle, with exaggerated and emphatic swinging of arms and hard-hitting feet. The step continues with a series of cracks on other fraternities, repeats the verse, and ends with two brothers escorting the woman back to the audience.)[32]

Figure 36. Alpha Phi Alpha mocks the Sigmas with "Your Mama Didn't Tell You 'bout A Phi A?" while circling a white female student and friend at Virginia Tech. (1983, photograph and video by Hazen Robert Walker)

This is a remarkable example of performance criticism embodied in performance. Step shows are full of meta-performances, that is, performances about performances, which focus attention on either the performance itself or on another performance and comment on it. Saluting steps imitate other performances in a positive way, but cracking steps are more critical. Both exhibit what Victor Turner terms "performative reflexivity," a condition in which "a sociocultural group, or its most perceptive members acting representatively, turn, bend or reflect back upon themselves, upon the relations, actions, symbols, meanings, codes, roles, statuses, social structures, ethical and legal rules, and other sociocultural components which make up their public 'selves.'"[33]

Cracking serves several functions among competing Greek organizations. First, it creates what Richard Bauman calls "differential identity."[34] That is, cracking defines a group's identity by contrasting it with other groups. Second, cracking is entertaining. It elicits laughter and howls of appreciation from the audience. If there is little competition between groups, cracking is taken lightly. But if there is intense competition cracking can create great tension. There was enormous rivalry between AKA and DST sororities during the mid–1980s at Virginia Tech, for example, and tensions became so severe that DST declined, for the first time, to step in the school's Overton R. Johnson Endowed Scholarship Step Competition in 1989. It was the only historically black Greek sorority that decided not to participate, culminating several years of tensions that revolved around cracks.

In 1986 an Alpha Kappa Alpha soror at Virginia Tech explained that "people like to listen to those [cracks]," but because of the "political atmosphere" on campus her sorority "[could not] do it without being cut up left and right. It's all-important to keep good relations with other fraternities and sororities," and "it's best for the time being that we don't say anything." During the same year, however, the fraternities were "just hav[ing] a good time cutting up."[35]

The third type of step, freaking or show dogging, exercises the need for individual identity within the group.[36] The freaker (or "show dog" as he or she is sometimes called) breaks the norm of synchronization and unity in an attempt at greater audience response (fig. 37). Although the main emphasis of stepping is to illustrate group solidarity and unity, occasional deviations from group synchronization assert freedom and the power of an individual to vary, in creative ways, from the group norm.

Figure 37. An Alpha Phi Alpha brother freaks or show dogs by breaking from the group formation in the crack step "We're Laughing at You" at Virginia Tech. (1983, photograph and video by Hazen Robert Walker)

Stepping at Festivals: The Philadelphia Greek Picnic

In addition to its role in the social drama of group maintenance, stepping has played an important role in annual festivals of black college students since the early 1970s. One of the largest and oldest of these festivals, the Philadelphia Greek Picnic, celebrated its twenty-fifth anniversary in 1999. Organized in 1974 by a small group of undergraduate Pan-Hellenic Council members who called themselves "The Family," the festival began in Blue Bell Park in the Germantown section of Philadelphia. In subsequent years it moved to the Belmont Plateau in Fairmont Park. By 1992 the Greek Picnic had attracted sixty thousand participants, and in 1999 the city of Philadelphia estimated that 250,000 would attend.[37]

McGregory has described Philadelphia Greek Picnic step shows as reflecting a highly spontaneous and carnivalesque atmosphere. She reported a "myriad of processions" and the "oceanic" effect of the "massive movement of cavorting lines, bounded by their own unifying orderly steps." Lively spontaneity still characterizes stepping at the Picnic. As Rita Harris quotes one soror at the 1999 event, "The greatest feeling in the world is to meet a

Soror that you've never met before from across the country, then you start singing, chanting, stepping, and partying together."[38]

Inverting social rules is common in carnivalesque settings, and the Greek Picnic is no exception. Fraternity members in the early 1990s inverted their roles of "preeminent gentlemen" by "conducting themselves like rogues." The traditional respect that they accord women "inverts into grotesquely sexist if not outright misogynistic behavior." For example, "a hoard of male revelers . . . were chanting, 'Shut Up, Bitch,'" from the lyrics of a popular rap song. Many women at the event "seem impervious to the indignities directed against them and seem to act with consenting symbolic collusion to this grotesque behavior." Despite the combination of heat, alcohol, and large crowds of young people, Greek Picnic has few acts of violence. One police officer said, "This is perfect, this is the best I've ever seen of any kind of rock concert or carnival."[39]

Crediting "impromptu stepping competitions" with keeping the peace, McGregory argued that they function as "ritual combat." The groups chant boasts about themselves and ridicule others. In the early 1990s, clowning behavior occurred in Greek Picnic step shows through the role of an "Omega man" who "emerge[d] annually as a clown figure." Dressed in "a tank top and running shorts in his fraternity's colors with a banner across his chest that [read]: 'Breastfeed me,'" he mimicked the spectators, even mooned the crowd, and was "equally prone to totally disrobing." This "public display of nudity suggests the powerful spirit of Carnival," McGregory observed.[40]

As the Philadelphia Greek Picnic has grown in size it has become highly organized and receives support from the city government and corporate sponsorship for a competitive step show. Minutemaid and Sprite, respectively, sponsored the 1998 and 1999 shows. A sophisticated and attractive Web-site <http://www.Phillygreek.com> advertises the event, and videotapes can be purchased via the Internet.

Newer events such as a family picnic, a college information row, and a job fair, have added to the Greek Picnic's respectability. Because it attracts many African Americans and the Philadelphia city government participates in planning the event, it has been open to the general public. The tensions between its origins as a black Greek event and its growing popularity with others have led to spirited discussion on the Internet about whether the Greek Picnic should be exclusively for members of black Greek letter organizations (BGLOs). Following violent acts that occurred in Philadelphia at the time of Greek Picnic but were not directly linked to the event, organizers decided to limit much of the 2000 and 2001 picnics to BGLO members.[41]

The Philadelphia Greek Picnic is reminiscent of another, earlier East Coast gathering of African Americans—the Pinkster Day celebrations that flourished in New York from the 1750s to the mid-nineteenth century. The annual Pinkster Festival, which lasted from three days to a week and allowed slaves more time off than at Christmas and New Year, became immensely popular. Dancing and dance competitions were an important part of the festivities, with juba dances being extremely popular. Patting juba, one of the early slave dances, reverberates in contemporary African American stepping (chapter 3). Although patting juba probably grew out of an African dance called *giouba,* it became "a special routine of slapping the hands, knees, thighs, and body in a rhythmic display," observe Marshall and Jean Stearns. Frederick Douglass describes the "juba beater" as "marking the words as he sang so as to have them fall pat with the movement of his hands."[42]

Reflecting and Creating Cultural Identity

Beyond its function in rites of passage and its role in the social drama of group maintenance, stepping expresses cultural identity in an artistic, compelling manner. As an oral tradition, stepping gains flexibility through the use of a wide variety of other traditional expressive forms and patterns such as call and response, rapping, the dozens, signifying, marking, spirituals, handclap games, and military chants ("jodies"). In addition, stepping movements, songs, and chants borrow from a long history of African American traditions, some deriving from slave and minstrel dances and others from such popular influences as tap, the lindy hop, the Florida A&M University band, black cheerleading, break dancing and hip-hop, military marching, and New Orleans street parades.[43] Embedded within these African American movement and communicative patterns are reflections of dance and communication patterns found in Africa.

The following four step routines use African American expressive traditions to build and display individual and group identity. The first is based on a military jody and call and response, the second uses rapping, the third uses call and response, and the fourth is based on children's handclap games. All four routines were performed in the mid–1980s outside a student dining hall at Virginia Tech. In most cases, I have chosen to transcribe the words and some paralinguistic features only, as well as general descriptions of the movement. In order to provide a full example of a step routine, however, I have transcribed both the words and movement to the synchronized handclap routine. Bold type indicates a louder, more emphatic tone of voice.

In "Do It on Two," a group of eight Alpha brothers lines up behind each other and begins an iambic step and clap punctuated by a loud, grunted

"Huah!" The leader in the front calls out, "Do it—huah!" and moves to one side of the group like a drill sergeant. He then yells out calls, accompanied by a step, which the group in the file imitates. The routine looks and sounds like a military jody, or marching chant, with a call and response pattern:

Leader: We're gonna roll it on out!
Group: We're gonna roll it on out!
Leader: We're gonna roll it on out!
Group: We're gonna roll it on out!
Leader: We're gonna do it on two!
Group: We're gonna do it on two!
Leader: We're gonna do it on two!
Group: We're gonna do it on two!
Leader: I say one!
Group: One!
Leader: I say two!
Group: Two![44]

"Clutch Me, Baby," from the same step show, is a rap that extols the sexual virtuosity of the Alphas. As in H. Rap Brown's well-known "Rap's Poem," the brothers employ double entendres and sexual metaphor. The group stands, single file, one behind the other. After the opening refrain, each member in turn moves to one side of the line and raps out a boast:

All: Oh clutch me baby,
　you doing okay
　for A Phi A.
　You're doing all right,
　you do it all night.
Leader (standing to one side):
　Clutch me baby,
　Marcus is my name,
　sex is my fame,
　'cause when my luck is right,
　I do it every night,
　'cause it's a smooth roman rocket
　that always hits your pocket.
All (refrain):
Second in line: Double-clutch me baby,
　my name is Rodney P,
　just bear with me a moment,
　I got a story, you see.

You said I like my women sweet
and I like them plump,
'cause all I want to do is the A Phi Hump.

(The step continues until each of the eight brothers has performed a rap.)[45]

A very common type of step routine is built on call and response, a prevalent African American communication pattern. In a 1986 show, AKA sisters stood in two rows facing the audience, with the stepmaster in the center of the front row. The stepmaster began a sultry, hip-swinging step and called out a series of questions, to which the sisters responded. This step is called the "Marcita" step, named after the woman who created it:

Leader: Sorors,
All: Ye-ah?
Leader: I said my sorors,
All: Ye-ah?
Leader: can we break it
All: Ye-ah?
Leader: on down now?
All: Yeah!

At the end of the last response, the group broke into a fast, complex step with intricate footwork that contrasted with the slow, sultry, hip-swinging step. They then returned to the slow hip swing for another call-response verse.[46]

Still another type of step imitates children's handclap games, an important motif of movement performance within African American culture, Friedland observes. "We got a lot of our chants" from street chants said an AKA soror at Virginia Tech in 1986. For example, they based one step routine on the rhythm of "just a little street chant":

Mama they would want to catch a clue in life
it might save them a whole lot of strife.
The lesson we teach is elementary
so see if you can understand what we mean.

We are the quality, we are the quantity,
we are the line of Theta Phi you see.
Your're green with envy,
we sense some jealousy,
because you didn't get to pledge our sorority.

Commenting on these chants, the Alpha Kappa Alpha soror said, "That just comes from something I know I used to say, like those little patty-cake games,

I *know* I used to play something to that effect." In stepping, "All you're really doing is taking old things and giving them a new twist."[47]

In 1986 Alpha Kappa Alpha at Virginia Tech performed a synchronized handclap routine reminiscent of children's games. Ten sisters faced the audience, then faced each other in two rows and advanced toward each other while doing a handclap routine. When the two rows met, they clapped with each other with the exaggerated, African American hand slap of greeting known as "giving skin." As they gave skin, they called out greetings in unison, such as "how you doing" and "sorors." To demonstrate unity, each member rotated down the row and around to the other side in a counterclockwise circle, so each clapped with and greeted everyone (fig. 38). In order to illustrate the intricate foot and hand work, a detailed text follows, with musical notation representing the rhythm of the hands and feet. The basic rhythm for all three steps is a 4/4 measure.[48]

Figure 38. The sisters of Alpha Kappa Alpha sorority "giving skin" in a synchronized handclap routine at Virginia Tech. (1986, photograph and video by Hazen Robert Walker)

This routine begins with eleven sisters facing the audience in a row, their hands clasped in front of their chests. Every other woman performs step one twice, while the others perform step two twice. Then the women switch steps. Those who performed step one now perform step two twice and vice versa. The entire group then performs step one nine times while moving backward and splitting into two parallel lines. The lines then move close together, facing each other, and the leader in the back of and between the two rows faces the audience. When they are in this position, the entire group performs step three twelve times, rotating with each repetition so each sister has given skin to each other and the leader has moved to the front of, and between, the two rows. The routine ends with the sisters facing the audience, frozen in the stance in which they began the number, their hands clasped in front of their chests (fig. 39.)

These four examples of steps illustrate stepping's power to incorporate such African American expressive traditions as military jodies, rapping, call and response, and children's handclap games. It is a highly flexible art form that employs numerous movement and vocal traditions to express cultural and group identity.

Conclusion

Stepping is an expressive performance art that also functions as a ritual of group identity. Whether it celebrates the rite of passage to brotherhood or sisterhood, enacts the social drama of group maintenance in black Greek-letter organizations, or celebrates African American cultural identity at annual festivals such as the Philadelphia Greek Picnic, stepping stimulates communitas among spectators and participants alike. The long hours of rehearsal necessary to synchronize intricate, complex movement patterns may create a physical entrainment among step team members that literally bears out the often-heard claim that people step to demonstrate unity.

Despite its function as a ritual, many steppers believe that the stepping tradition is directly linked to their African heritage. They view it as a way to express their African identity. As Valerie Warnsby, a DST sorority member from Drake University in Des Moines, Iowa, observes, "All day we're bombarded with stuff from white America. For us, it's an artistic expression of our history."[49] Just how that history manifests itself in stepping is the subject of the next chapter.

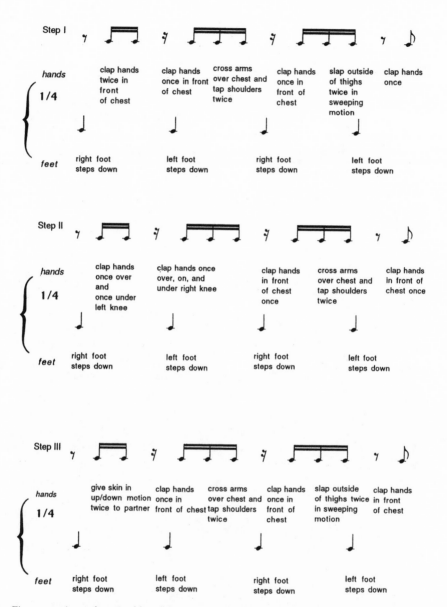

Figure 39. A synchronized handclap routine as performed by Alpha Kappa Alpha sorority, Virginia Tech, 1986.

3 / Stepping Out an African Heritage

Deep in my heart
I love Africa.
I love, I love, I love,
my Africa.
—Step Afrika! USA, Kennedy Center, Washington D.C.,
23 January 2000

Claims for the African roots of stepping are widespread and appear in many different contexts. In 1997, when emcee Tyrone Petty introduced the first large Christian step show in the District of Columbia area, he explained, "It was commonplace in the tribes of Africa to use dance in all of their lives. It was part of wedding ceremonies, it was part of funeral ceremonies, it was a part of religious ceremonies." Stepping was "just taking it back and putting in proper focus . . . that which was ours to begin with." In 1994 a Christian step team in Detroit, Michigan, chanted, "Africa is where stepping began, from the beat of the drums to the sound of our feet." Alphonso Ribiero, emcee of the 1993 televised *S.T.O.M.P.* competition, alluded to South African gumboot dancing when he said, "Others insist that stepping was started by miners in South Africa. It was a clever way to communicate while they knocked the dirt from their boots after a long day in the coal mines." In 1990, AKA sisters at the University of South Florida in Tampa also claimed that stepping originated in African dance traditions. Stepping "goes all the way back to African culture," when different tribes would show their competition through dance maintained an AKA soror at Virginia Tech in 1986.[1]

Indeed, competitive tribal dancing in African cultures is well known. In the West African country of Benin, for example, people participate in a monthly dance called *avogan* in which young men and women from different quarters of a city take turns satirizing their rivals: "Much prestige goes to those who live in the same quarter as the composers whose songs bite deepest into the shortcomings of their rivals, and thereby become the popular hits of the city at large."[2]

Despite the many claims of stepping's African origins, not all agree. Michael Gordon, former executive director of the NPHC, pledged the Alpha Phi chapter of Kappa Alpha Psi at Virginia State University in 1955. He says that he "disappoints a lot of young brothers" when he tells them that during this period "there was no great Afrocentric movement." Indeed, Gordon recalls, "especially in the historically black colleges during that period, Africa was the last thing that people tried to identify with." Although there "were certain individual people who were a little more advanced than others who cared about or knew about African history and maybe admired W. E. B. Du Bois, . . . most young black people in the colleges in the 1950s were trying to be upwardly mobile and accepted in the mainstream of American society." Gordon acknowledges that the stepping of that period reflected African movements, such as an African American way of walking, as well as African American songs, such as the spirituals from which many fraternity and sorority songs borrowed their tunes, but maintains that steppers did not self-consciously imitate African movements. Not until the early 1970s at Howard University did Gordon encounter "Omega Psi Phi men who deliberately put on certain movements that recalled their African heritage. And I remember being thrilled at seeing that."[3]

Confirming Gordon's assessment that steppers in earlier years did not associate their activities with African influences, Darryl R. Matthews, Sr., a former executive director of Alpha Phi Alpha who pledged in the Delta Rho chapter at the University of Missouri at Kansas City in 1972, wrote in an e-mail debate with a younger brother:

> When my big brothers did it in the 60's, it was to the doo-wopping style of the r&b artist of the day. There was nothing deliberately African about that. In the 70's we modeled ourselves after the Temptations and the Dramatics. It was syncopated harmony with show business choreography, pure and simple. It was not about anything African.
>
> We did not know anything about this side of Africa. We only knew of the British imposed colonial imperialism and the revolutionaries who were trying to free their physically and mentally enslaved countrymen. To say we were stepping to relate to Mother Africa is disingenuous and inaccurate.
>
> No news, art, dances, nothing was getting in or out of South Africa so we did not know anything about rubber boot dancing. That is recently discovered phenomena. I guess y'all young folks had the serious hook up on the goings on inside of the formerly apartheid-ridden regime. Nobody else did, and there was no CNN in those days.[4]

The rubber boot or gumboot dancing to which Matthews refers is an excellent example of the complex relationships between African and African American music and dance. Gumboot dancing (*isicathulo*), one of the first urban working-class dances in South Africa, may have been developed in rural missions by Zulu pupils who were not allowed to perform traditional dances. The word *isicathulo*, Hugh Tracey notes, means "shoe." When the students danced, the shoes that missions required them to wear created louder sounds than did bare feet. Around the time of World War I, "rural, urban, mission, and working-class performance traditions" intermingled in isicathulo, which "as a step dance" was "closely related if not identical with other dance forms that had evolved earlier among farm laborers and inhabitants of the rural reserves."[5]

Erlmann suggests that isicathulo dancers "frequently indulge in sophisticated solo stepping, prototypes of which had been available to migrant workers from the mid–1920s through Charlie Chaplin and Fred Astaire movies as well as touring black tap dance groups." Indeed, South Africans were exposed to African American music and dance traditions as early as 1890, when Orpheus M. McAdoo and the Virginia Jubilee Singers spent almost five years touring South Africa. In subsequent years, black South Africans came to the United States. One, the famous "ragtime" composer Reuben T. Caluza, renowned "as a skilled *isicathulo* dancer," enrolled in Virginia's Hampton Institute in 1930 to earn a B.A. in music. Caluza and three other students from Africa formed the African Quartette (fig. 40), performing both songs and dances along the East Coast. They even sang for Franklin D. Roosevelt. Quartette member Dwight Sumner wrote that in their summer tour of 1931 the "African Quartette sang Zulu songs, under the direction of Mr. Caluza, and also gave African folk dances." It is likely that Caluza shared his talents with students. If so, members of fraternities and sororities could have incorporated some gumboot movements into stepping. Caluza went on to earn a master's degree at Columbia University in 1935, where again he could have shared gumboot dancing with students.[6]

Malone notes that during the 1970s and 1980s gumboot dancing "was introduced in North American urban areas and showcased by many of the dance companies that performed styles of traditional African dances." Evidence from Erlmann, however, suggests the possibility of a much earlier American exposure to gumboot dancing and, conversely, the incorporation of African American influences into South African dances. Caluza's story is only one small example of the continuous interactions among Africans and African Americans that created a complex interaction between music and dance forms on both continents. The founding director of the Soweto Dance

Figure 40. Reuben T. Caluza, second from right, and members of the African Quartette. (Courtesy of Hampton University Archives)

Theatre, Jackie Semela, explains that just as South Africans were influenced in their music and dance by touring performers from the United States such as Duke Ellington, so, too, did South Africans display their own dances: "And wherever South Africans travel, they would always show a gumboot dance, they would also show a Zulu dance, they would also show some tradition of South Africa in some of their songs" (fig. 41). Semela agrees that there is a "likelihood" that Caluza's interactions with black people in colleges in the United States could have brought a gumboot influence to stepping.[7]

Thus, it is impossible to argue that "pure" African dances directly influenced African American stepping, because the same popular culture traditions that were influencing stepping in America might also have been influencing African dances. As James Clifford observes, identities in the twentieth century "no longer presuppose continuous cultures or traditions. Everywhere individuals and groups improvise local performances from (re)collected pasts, drawing on foreign media, symbols, and languages." The more recent work of Step Afrika! to exchange American, U.K., and Afri-

Figure 41. Jackie Semela of the Soweto Dance Theatre teaches the South African gum-boot dance at a Step Afrika! step clinic at the Kennedy Center in Washington, D.C., January 2000. (Photograph by Hazen Robert Walker)

can dance traditions in an annual international festival in Johannesburg has only heightened the intercultural mixture of movement traditions (chapter 5). The step team of the D.C. Coalition of Alpha Phi Alpha, Inc., has used "Dun-Dun-Bah," a West African dance from Guinea, as well as Zulu dances from South Africa in their step shows, Jeff Johnson reports.[8]

Some movement patterns in stepping may have been conscious adoptions of African dance patterns, but it is more likely that movement and communicative patterns from Africa came with the first black immigrants and slaves who adapted those patterns to their new North American environment. A people who had highly developed verbal, musical, and dance traditions in their various cultures would surely find some way to continue them in new contexts, especially when they offered psychological release from the horrors of slavery. These African traditions melded with traditions from other cultures to create the distinctive African American expressive genres found in stepping.

Patting Juba and Ring Shouts

The characteristic clapping and stomping movements of stepping have their earliest counterparts in African American dances that emerged during slavery. Patting juba, perhaps the best-known of these dances, may have originated in an African dance called *guiouba* and grown in popularity after slaveholders outlawed drums among slaves for fear they would be used to communicate revolts. Solomon Northup describes the dance as "striking the hands on the knees, then striking the hands together, then striking the right shoulder with one hand, the left with the other—all the while keeping time with the feet, and singing." Lewis Paine's 1851 description comments on how patting juba was used to provide "music" by which to dance:

> Some one calls for a fiddle—but if one is not to be found some one "pats juber." This is done by placing one foot a little in advance of the other, raising the ball of the foot from the ground, and striking it in regular time, while, in connection, the hands are struck slightly together, and then upon the thighs. In this way they make the most curious noise, yet in such perfect order, it furnishes music to dance by. . . . It is really astonishing to witness the rapidity of their motions, their accurate time, and the precision of their music and dance. I have never see it equaled in my life.[9]

The juba step was often done in a counterclockwise circle, with "both the words and the steps" in call-and-response form. It involved improvization, the shuffle, and clapping, all "major Afro-American traits," as Marshall and Jean Stearns have noted. "The two men in the center start the performance with the Juba step while the surrounding men clap, and then switch to whatever new step is named in the call, just before the response 'Juba! Juba!' sounds and the entire circle starts moving again." The counterclockwise circular motion is common to rituals in the Kongo culture, from which one-third of U.S. blacks derived, and symbolizes the "circle of the sun about the earth."[10]

Minstrel dancers featured patting juba. Perhaps the best of all African American minstrels, William Henry Lane ("Master Juba"), earned a reputation as "the greatest dancer of them all" by 1845. Because Lane performed in the "dance dives" of the Five Points district in Lower Manhattan, a place of tenements that housed both Irish immigrants and blacks, it was inevitable that he, like other African Americans, would blend African dance elements with Irish jigs. Gradually, people adopted the term *jigs* to describe "the general style" of African American dancing. Thus, just as stepping has incorporated African influences, it may have picked up European influences as well.[11]

Early circular stepping routines reflect the influence of patting juba as well as another early African American dance, the ring shout, which still exists in small areas of the South. A true ring shout consisted "of movement in a circle with the feet never crossed and usually not lifted from the ground, accompanied by a vocal 'band' composed of lead singer and 'basers' who sang only religious texts; it flourished in the Sea Islands and the adjoining coastal region, the area of the distinctive Gullah dialect." Baptists as well as many other evangelical Christian groups believed that dancing was sinful, but, Stearns and Stearns note, because "Baptists defined dancing as a crossing of legs, the Ring Shout was considered acceptable."[12]

Although ring shouts were part of black religious services, they also occurred in secular contexts—in schools and homes and among black soldiers—and were popular with adults as well as children. Charlotte Forten, a black teacher among the freedmen on the Sea Islands in 1862, describes the "shouts" that children performed:

> In the evening, the children frequently came in to sing and shout for us. These "shouts" are very strange,—in truth, almost indescribable. It is necessary to hear and see in order to have any clear idea of them. The children form a ring, and move around in a kind of shuffling dance, singing all the time. Four or five stand apart, and sing very energetically, clapping their hands, stamping their feet, and rocking their bodies to and fro. These are the musicians, to whose performance the shouters keep perfect time. The grown people on this plantation did not shout, but they do on some of the other plantations.[13]

Although many accounts of ring shouts describe shuffling steps, the diary of Thomas Wentworth Higginson, a colonel in the first black regiment to be called into service in the Civil War, records a variety of steps performed by soldiers of the First Regiment, South Carolina Volunteers. At dusk on 3 December 1862, for example, they gathered around fires built inside a "sort of little booth made neatly of palm leaves covered in at top, a native African hut in short." The men sang "at the top of their voices, . . . all accompanied with a regular drumming of the feet & clapping of the hands, like castenets." Then, as "the excitement [spread]":

> [Men] outside the enclosure begin to quiver & dance, others join, a circle forms, winding monotonously round some one in the centre. Some heel & toe tumultuously, others merely tremble & stagger on, others stoop & rise, others whirl, others caper sidewise all keep steadily circling like dervishes, outsiders applaud especial strokes of skill, my approach only enlivens the scene, the circle enlarges, louder grows the singing about Jesus & Heaven, & the ceaseless drumming & clapping go steadily on. At last seems to come a snap and the spell breaks amid general sighs & laughter. And this not rarely & occasionally but night after night.[14]

An African Aesthetic in Stepping

Although stepping bears striking resemblances to the early dances of ring shouts and patting juba, it also powerfully embodies aesthetic elements widely recognized in the music and dance of Western and Central Africa. In 1966 Robert Farris Thompson identified five common features of West African music and dance: percussive dominance, multiple meter, apart playing and dancing, call and response, and songs and dances of derision. Expanding his study to include Central Africa in *African Art in Motion* (1974), Thompson compared native African aesthetic criticism with that of outside, academic observers. He identified ten "canons of fine form" in African art and dance. Many are highly visible in African American stepping.[15]

Thompson argues that both African art and dance prize youthful vitality and that "without vital aliveness we are no longer talking about African art." Applying the argument to dance, Thompson writes, "People in Africa, regardless of their actual age, return to strong, youthful patterning whenever they move within the streams of energy which flow from drums or other sources of percussion. They obey the implications of vitality with the music and its speed and drive." Three other aspects of African art and dance convey this youthful power. The first, to "swing every note and every color strong" calls for "phrasing every note and step with consummate vitality." The second, "vital aliveness" or "playing the body parts with percussive strength," not only involves powerful percussive force but also leads to multiple meter and the "interpretation of the parts of the body as independent instruments of percussive force." Thus, a stepper may throw down a sharply percussive rhythm with her feet while her hands beat out a counter rhythm and her head sharply enunciates yet another beat. Thompson's observation that "vital aliveness, high intensity, speed, drive—these are some of the facets of artful muscularity and depth of feeling that characterize the dances of this continent" could just as easily be applied to African American stepping.[16]

Indeed, youthful vitality might also be expressed as a quality of "hot," which works in opposition to the aesthetic of cool maintains Alicia J. Rouverol. She finds this "hot" quality expressed through a rapid and intense form of stepping called "hard-stepping," which is used to heighten audience response. Hard stepping works to "elevate" a routine, much as gospel singers add improvisational segments to reach a strong climax. A third trait that conveys youthfulness is "flexibility." "Dance with bended knees," the Kongo say, "lest you be taken for a corpse." A young Luba dancer in Kinshasa told Thompson that a Luba must "manifest his suppleness with bent knees, bent elbows, and suave oscillations to the music." The posture of bent knees and bent elbows is one of the most common stances that steppers use.[17]

Because steppers use several parts of their bodies as percussive instruments they can develop sophisticated, complex rhythmic patterns that embody two of Thompson's canons of an African aesthetic: simultaneous suspending and preserving of the beat and multiple meter. Just as African musicians frequently suspend the beat in order to insert accented, melodic tones, steppers often produce a syncopated rhythm as they play with the timing of the beat to create complex rhythmic patterns. One stepper alone may create multiple meter or polyrhythm. Within a group of steppers, each performer might perform different clapping and stepping patterns so that a contrapuntal rhythmic fugue emerges. Musicologists have long observed that "African music is distinguished from other world traditions by the superimposition of several lines of meter." Part of the great appeal of stepping may lie in its difference from European-based musical traditions, which have "at any one moment one rhythm in command," whereas "a piece of African music has always two or three, sometimes as many as four." As the Phi Beta Sigma chapter at Virginia Tech describe their stepping style, "Sigmas utilize virtually every part of their anatomy to produce soulful, syncopated rhythms. Sigma stepping at its best is speed, precision, and complication."[18]

To increase the complexity and audibility of percussive sounds, stepping groups often use canes or sticks to beat out rhythms. Similar use of sticks and canes is used by such African cultures as the Mbuti and Zulu and by groups from northern Zaire, Sudan, Zambia, and Mozambique, Malone asserts. Abrahams notes that African American slaves preferred to dance on wooden planks so they could better hear the polyrhythmic sounds. Clearly, an appreciation of strong, percussive beats unites stepping with earlier African American and African dance traditions.[19]

One of the most striking stances that African American steppers assume is best described as the "get-down" position. Steppers often begin and end a step by bending deeply from the waist so their torsos are at an almost forty-five-degree angle to the ground. From this stance they may swing their arms out sharply in front of them or to the side. Even in the midst of a step routine, steppers often bend their knees deeply and move low to the ground. Noting the importance of getting down, the Sigma Doves, Phi Beta Sigma's sweetheart organization, chanted "stepping real hard / and stooping real low / the Sigma Doves / are going to put on a show" during the 1985 Blue and White Weekend at the University of Florida. Many Central and West African cultures consider dancing low to the ground to be virtuosic and symbolize "a dual expression of salutation and devotion," Thompson observes.

"Get-down sequences" show "honor and respect, either to a fine drummer, in response to the savor of his phrasing, or to a deity." In some cases, a get-down posture coincides with the point in the performance at which a dancer shows greatest vigor and intensity. Thus it, too, conveys youthful vitality and, as Rouverol argues, may also indicate a hot rather than a cool aesthetic quality.[20]

In contrast to the hot power of a get-down stance combined with the youthful intensity of multiple meter and hard-stepping, African American steppers exhibit the African aesthetic of the cool, an aesthetic and philosophical concept that unites all other aesthetic canons. In Africa, maintains Thompson, "coolness is an all-embracing positive attribute which combines notions of composure, silence, vitality, healing, and social purification." Five qualities contribute to the aesthetic of the cool: visibility, luminosity, smoothness, rebirth and reincarnation, and facial composure (the "mask of the cool" as Thompson observes). All these features appear, in varying degrees, in stepping. Perhaps the most noticeable is Thompson's mask of the cool, when steppers' composed, serene faces contrast with their intricate and powerful percussive movements.[21]

Steppers also strive for visibility or clarity in their motions and voices; indeed, judges of competitions often look for those attributes. Thus, bodily movements are sharp, crisp, and emphatic. Step teams often exhibit appreciation for luminosity or brilliance through the bright colors they wear as well as the ways they use spotlights and strobes to intensify their movements. Another "function of perfected clarity" is smoothness, which Thompson identifies as a "unified aesthetic impact" in which "seams do not show." Step teams pride themselves on displaying unity through synchronized, carefully rehearsed movements. In competitions, judges often deduct points for lapses in unity.[22]

A more philosophical way of invoking coolness comes through Thompson's concept of rebirth and reincarnation, which overlaps with his category of ancestorism. The categories are related, and both are particularly important in the secular stepping of Greek-letter organizations as well as the sacred stepping of religious groups. Fraternities and sororities often invoke the names or the number of their founders (e.g., Alpha Phi Alpha's "Seven Jewels"), especially when they perform retrospective steps that commemorate group history. Likewise, religious steppers often invoke biblical passages for the text of a routine. In both cases, such references connect the current moment of stepping to venerated people and words from the past. Thompson contends that pleasure derived from the "motion arts" in Africa comes "because many people see the founders of the nation or lineage returning in these styles." Through the dances, they are participating "in an alternative, ancient, far superior universe."[23]

Stepping also has the power to link both audience and performers to important images and ideas from the group's shared history. In their 1995 spring step show, for example, the Omega Psi Phi brothers at Virginia Tech performed a retrospective routine dedicated to the four founders of their fraternity. The stepmaster began each of the four verses of the routine by saying that if Oscar J. Cooper, Frank Coleman, Edgar A. Love, and Ernest E. Just were there they "would do a little step that goes like this." Each of the three other steppers then demonstrated a different step and kept performing it during subsequent verses. By the last verse, each of the four was performing a different step but in unison, demonstrating not only the variety of steps in their repertoire but also the ability to maintain their own rhythm and form. At the same time, they demonstrated virtuosity in having mastered a key feature of African dance and music tradition—multiple meter or cross rhythm.[24]

One of the most notable aspects of step shows is the concern steppers give to their appearance. Step teams pay great attention to their dress and keep their uniforms for competitive shows secret until the public appearance. "Looking smart," Thompson notes, is the African English phrase used to praise dancers who make a good impression. As Thompson defines it, looking smart involves "strikingly attractive use of style, loaded with notions of preening and the making of the person sexually attractive." Judges of the Overton R. Johnson Step Competition at Virginia Tech use the criteria of execution (precision, technique, and synchronization); appearance; vocalization; crowd appeal; and personality. Thus, it is not surprising that groups would give so much attention to looking smart, because it has great bearing on three of the five criteria for excellence. At Howard University, Malone observes, "dress is always an important part of the planning process," and sororities and fraternities pay "close attention to the types of fabrics selected and the heaviness and sound quality of the shoes."[25]

The clothes worn by a fraternity or sorority step team usually indicate the group's colors and are often metaphors for group identity. In the 1986 Overton R. Johnson Step Competition, Alpha Kappa Alpha chose green taffeta, knee-length dresses with puffy, short sleeves. They accessorized with matching green garters and high heels. The outfits were in keeping with the refined, feminine image that AKA sorors cultivate and with their routines, which in that show included a great deal of singing and dancing to music. In the same competition, Delta Sigma Theta wore white tuxedos and gloves, along with red cummerbunds, boutonnieres, bow ties, half-masks, and high heels. Not only did their outfit display the sorority's red and white colors, but it also conveyed concern for showmanship, style, and glitz and allowed freedom of movement for intricate hard stepping.[26]

While attention to dress helps make a group "look smart," so do two other African aesthetic qualities: a "correct entrance and exit" and "personal and representational balance." Teams work hard to capture the audience's attention through innovative and memorable entrances and exits. Groups that perform on stages equipped with curtains, lights, and sound systems might use special props, lighting, and sound effects. Omega Psi Phi, for example, won first place in the 1987 Overton R. Johnson Step Competition with what one brother described as "something new and different":

> Agent ooQ, briefcase in hand and clad in a tan trench coat, stands before a female spy wearing sunglasses and carrying a portable stereo. He exchanges his briefcase for the cassette player then turns it on and listens for his mission.
>
> A voice booms over the box describing, in detail, six men known collectively as the "deadliest stepping brothers in VPI history," slide shots of the six brothers flash on a nearby projection screen as the voice lists their names and aliases, also known as "dog names."
>
> Six men emerge from behind a black curtain to the beat of Herb Alpert's song, "Keep Your Eye on Me" while the Burruss Auditorium crowd cheers wildly. The men of Omega Psi Phi fraternity are ready to step.[27]

Groups frequently enter to popular music, often performing what black fraternities and sororities label "party walks" and what Latino Greek organizations call "strolls." Malone defines a party walk as an "organized line movement performed around the floor at a party." Party walks and strolls may or may not include the characteristic stomping and clapping of stepping, but they are performed to music.[28]

In addition to crowd-captivating entrances and exits, steppers define routines by doing what Thompson calls "cutting the dance," "killing the song," or establishing "clear boundaries" around each. Just as the Yoruba say that "dancers must prepare for the opening beat of the dance before moving—like a boxer, bracing for the punch" and the Luba and Tiv "demand that a dancer determine the position of his body, as a quasi-sculptural force with bent knees and arms held close to the trunk, before actually dancing," African American steppers launch into a stepping routine from a position of stasis. To borrow a term used in classical art criticism to describe the representation of motion, the characteristic resting pose could be called a "rhythmos" ("shape" or "pattern"). The term *rhythmos* was derived from the "momentary stops" in dancing called "eremiai," in which a body is "held for an instant in characteristic positions." One such stop was called a "rhyth-mos." Ancient Greeks used the term to refer to the pose of sculpture that conveys the expectation of movement. Thus, Myron's classic statue Diskobo-los (the Discus Thrower) depicts an athlete, coiled tightly, a moment before he throws his discus.[29]

Similarly, except for their entrance onstage, steppers begin from some position of rest, often a position that anticipates motion. In one common stance they stand at attention, heads held high and arms bent, clenched fists resting in front of or under their chins. In another typical stance they bend forward at the waist at a forty-five-degree angle to the ground and with both arms extended to one side. In the former case, one anticipates that the arms will swing free; in the latter, that the torso will spring up. Anticipation builds as the steppers use the moment of repose to catch their breath, focus their attention, and listen for the stepmaster's cues to begin the next routine.

Just as a step routine emerges from a quiet rhythmos, it ends with anoth-er rhythmos. Thompson writes that the Akan "strike moralistic poses."[30] Frequently the final poses of a step routine are symbolic as well. Often rou-tines end with members forming their group's hand signals. During the 1999 Latino Greek Summer Step and Stroll Show in the Bronx, a Lambda Upsi-lon Lambda fraternity step team ended a step with a remarkable rhythmos that called for great poise because the steppers were standing, balanced on one leg. The pose, a variation of Rodin's *The Thinker*, mimed a sitting po-sition, one leg crossed and resting on the other knee, elbow resting on the elevated knee, and chin on folded hand. The fingers of both hands formed the fraternity's hand signal (fig. 42). The steppers assumed the pose at the end of a chanted step:

> I looked to the sky
>   and what did I see?
> I saw the thirteen knights
>   looking down at me.
> They took my hand
>   and said "understand
> you're a brother
> like no other.
> You're a Lambda man" (*knee-elbow-chin pose*).[31]

Such a pose is certainly in keeping with the up-scale image of Lambda Upsilon Lambda fraternity, which has chapters at six of the seven Ivy League colleges. The pose is not unique to Lambda Upsilon Lambda, however. In 1986 Alpha Phi Alpha, also known for having an intellectual image, used a

Figure 42. Striking a final pose or rhythmos at the end of a routine, a Lambda Upsilon Lambda fraternity step team adopts a reflective stance. (Photograph by Hazen Robert Walker)

similar one in the Overton R. Johnson Step Competition. In 1985 at the University of Florida's Blue and White Weekend the Sigma Doves used a slight variation to illustrate "we're number one." Instead of resting their chins on their hands, they held up pointed index fingers in front of their chins.[32]

Striking a one-legged pose is unusual and crowd-pleasing because doing so deviates from the typical emphasis on what Thompson calls "personal and representational balance." Both in African art and dance, the human image "rises, in the main, from feet set flat and firm upon the earth." Thompson quotes Bessie Jones and Beth Lomax Hawes, who compared differences in the dances of mainland whites and Sea Island blacks: "All [black] dancing is done flat-footed; this is extremely difficult for [white] Americans, whose first approach to a dancing situation is to go up on their toes." While West Africans "cultivate divinity through richly stabilized traditions of personal balance," Thompson notes, the convention of balance would "doubtless soon wax boring, were it not honored so magnificently in the breach by kicks, spins, and leaps of certain of the men's dances in Africa."[33] Although most ending and beginning stances express the strong African emphasis on equilibrium, occasionally breaking the norm makes a step routine stand out.

The interrelated African canons of call and response and "apart dancing" are prominent in African American step shows. The first, call and response, embodies the important step team goal of expressing group unity. The pervasive antiphonal structure of call and response within African American expressive arts is familiar to many people. From the dynamic interactions of traditional black preachers and their congregations, to work songs, the blues, and jazz, the concept of a leader calling out and a chorus responding seems omnipresent. In stepping, too, many chants and steps have a call-and-response structure (chapter 2). In sub-Saharan Africa, notes Thompson, not only words and song but also dance take on a call-and-response structure, and "solo-and-circle, or solo-and-line, or solo-and-solo forms of dancing mirror melodic call-and-response."[34]

Call and response in dance reveals another characteristic of African dance, apart dancing, in which participants maintain separate spaces rather than have the sustained body contact seen in Western couple dancing. But dancing apart does not mean there is no unity. Rather, apartness fosters a dialogue between dancers as they call and respond with both voice and body. As Thompson says, "West Africans perform music and dance apart the better to ensure a dialog between movement and sound."[35]

Beneath the aesthetic use of call and response lies a significant message: "perfected social interaction." Call and response, Thompson observes, is "a danced judgment of qualities of social integration and cohesion." In Africa, a performer who disappoints the audience will find their responses "growing progressively weaker until they ultimately reform about a man with stronger themes and better aesthetic organization." Audiences of African American step shows judge the cohesiveness and unity of a group in part by the level of enthusiasm and responsiveness demonstrated through call and response. Not only do performers call and respond to each other, but also the audience responds and calls out in dynamic interchange as the steppers play to it. For example, references to a particular fraternity or sorority will often stimulate audience members affiliated with that group to shout out a group call such as "skee wee" or "nupe, nupe." As Amy Davis attests, "Steppers are greeted either with applause and cheers of support throughout a routine, or if they lose the audience's respect and attention, murmurs and unnerving quiet."[36]

The preceding canons of good form in African art and dance have focused on stylistic features, but a final characteristic, dances of derision, deals with content rather than style and, as Thompson maintains, plays a moral function. Throughout Western, Central, and Southern Africa, people use songs of allusion and dances of derision to make moral judgments on the behavior of others. Frequently, a fraternity or sorority will perform chants that define its ethos in opposition to that of its competitors. Through cracking on rivals, groups elevate their own images, as the Alpha Phi Alpha brothers at East Tennessee State University in Johnson City did in a classic step entitled "King Tut":

> *All:* My-y-y old King Tut
> was the very first Greek,
> a-a-h, when he clapped his hands
> he had the ladies at his feet.
> A-a-h, Tut, Tut, Tut,
> a-a-h, Tut, Tut, Tut.
>
> *One brother:* I said
>
> *All:* When he saw the Sigmas,
> it made him mad.
> When he saw the Kappas,
> it made him mad.
> A-a-h, when he saw the Ques,
> it made him sick.
> When he saw the frat,
> then he had to pledge it quick.
> A-ah, Tut, Tut, Tut,
> a-a-h, Tut, Tut, Tut.
> He had a black and gold whip
> and a black and gold cane,
> then he came up
> a-a-h with this black and gold name.
> A-ha-h A Phi A,
> A Phi A,
> A Phi A.[37]

The popularity of crack steps stems from the strong emphasis on competition in both African and African American verbal art and dance. Competition pervaded such early plantation dances among slaves as the cakewalk and the chalk-line walk. At set dances and buck dances at neighborhood frolics in Georgia during the early 1900s, the best dancers were rewarded with special clothing.[38] Twentieth-century dances such as tap, the lindy, the jitterbug, and break dancing have all involved competitions. Moreover, the verbal duels of the dozens (also called sounding and snapping), rapping, and signifying encourage quick wit and oral skill, bringing elevated social prestige to those who can best their peers.[39]

Conclusion

The syncopated, percussive hand-slapping and foot-stomping movements in stepping reveal their descent from early African American dances such as patting juba and ring shouts. The outlawing of drums among slaves may have heightened the development of percussive slapping and stomping as substitutes for drumbeats. Stepping also exhibits the key aesthetic features found in Western and Central African cultures as delineated by Robert Farris Thompson. The first Africans who came to North America brought their dance, movement, and musical traditions with them; in North America, they blended with other cultural influences, such as Irish step dancing. Winning competitions with Irish jig dancers, the famous African American minstrel William Henry Lane combined both African and Irish step dancing. Gradually, the most popular term to describe the general style of African American dancing became *jigs*. Stepping has African roots, but it also bears European influences.

After the Civil War, cultural exchanges between musical performers from Africa and the United States created a two-way flow of African and African American influences. Traveling black American minstrel shows brought spirituals and dances such as the cakewalk to Africa. Dances in American films influenced South African gumboot dancers during the 1920s and 1930s, and traveling groups of African singers and dancers such as Reuben T. Caluzo's African Quartette may have inspired African Americans to copy some of their movement patterns. Even though steppers in the 1950s and 1960s may not have consciously adopted an African style or expressed solidarity with African cultures, they expressed elements of an African aesthetic through stepping. As Afrocentrism grew in popularity during the 1970s, steppers began to articulate the connections they saw between the art of stepping and African culture.

Understanding the attitudes of black secret societies toward African culture in the early part of the twentieth century requires more investigation. If, as Malone argues, some members of the earliest black American secret societies of the eighteenth century were "either born in Africa or were one generation removed from the continent" and shared Central and West Africa concerns for proper burials, mutual aid, and economic cooperation, then it is possible that these African values continued in the mutual aid societies in existence when the first black Greek organizations were founded.[40] Because elaborate parades and drill team competitions were important activities of these societies at the beginning of the twentieth century, it is likely that early members of the first black Greek-letter organizations may have modeled their ritual of marching on line after such traditions.

By the 1990s the African American steppers of Step Afrika! had linked forces with dancers in South Africa and the United Kingdom to use the dance traditions of Africa, the Caribbean, and the United Kingdom to foster intercultural dialogue. Such intense international dance exchanges may heighten contemporary African influences on African American stepping.

4 / Stepping Forth: New Participants and Venues

When I think about Jesus, and what he's done for me,
when I think about Jesus, and how he set me free,
I want to step, step, step, step, step, step, step.
—Alpha Omega Christian Steppers, Metropolitan Baptist
Church, Washington, D.C.

The day before Easter on a sunny afternoon in Washington, D.C., in 1997, a crowd filled the Theodore Roosevelt High School auditorium to see the largest Christian step show ever held in the city. Sponsored by Marsha Sumner Ministries, Inc., and billed as "A Christian Step Show and FUN-draiser," the event featured thirteen Christian step teams from the metropolitan area. Some were from churches, such as Troop GOD from the First Baptist Church of Guilford and the Order My Steps Ministry from the Mt. Sinai Baptist Church. Others were from schools, such as AAMEN (the African American Male Educational Network) from the St. Francis Xavier School, South East, and the Soldiers of the Redeemed from the Academy of the Redeemed. Still other teams called themselves community-based, such as the Young Steppers for Christ. One, the Living Daily with the Scriptures Drill Team from the Star of Bethlehem Church of God in Christ (COGIC), reflected the influence of African American drill team traditions. What united all the groups was their commitment to stepping as a form of Christian witnessing and worship.

Indeed, the event had the aspect of a church service. Performers stepped opening prayers, scriptures, and spirituals; participants exchanged call-and-response praises; a band played contemporary gospel; ushers collected an offering; and the emcees issued a call to fellowship and even an altar call at the end. Banners above the stage read "Jesus Saves," "Marsha Sumner Ministries, Incorporated, " and "Youth in Praise Holy Ghost Throw Down."

Before the show began, Tyrone Petty, the main emcee, called all steppers to the stage to review the rules with them and lead them in prayer.

A member of the first group to step, Alpha Omega Delta, Christian Fellowship Sorority, Inc., pointed out how their stepping differed from that of black Greek sororities as she introduced their first step, a syncopated version of John 3:16:

> I want to thank you and say welcome to this Christian Step Show showcase. We are here not to compete, not to say these are our colors [displayed the t-shirt she wore that had Greek lettering], you're not a part. . . . That is not what we're out here for. We're out here because this is a mission. This is our mission. To step for God. To show you that God is the head of our lives. We're not here to say, oh, she's an AKA, so she can't do this, and she's a Delta Sigma Theta, so she can't be a part of us. That has nothing to do with it. Does anybody know why God died? Does anybody? Does anybody know? He died— , I say one of the reasons that he died was because God loved us, and we're going to do a step that says that "God loved us." And it goes:

For
God
so
loved
the world
that he gave
his only begotten (*stomp*)
son
his only begotten (*stomp*)
son
that whosoever believeth in him
that whosoever believeth in him
shall not perish
but have
e—v er la—st ing life.[1]

Near the end of the event Tyrone Petty said, "Now, we are watching a revolutionary movement of a step into our churches."[2] Although stepping had occurred as a part of Christian ministries in the District of Columbia area as early as 1992, the 1997 event was the first citywide show. It demonstrated the growing popularity and visibility of stepping in new contexts, for new audiences, and new purposes. What began as the ritual of secret societies and gestated on college campuses for half a century is gaining increasing popularity among a mass audience and in such off-campus sites as churches, schools, and community organizations. Stepping has even spread to Latino, Asian, and multicultural fraternities and sororities.

Stimuli for the Spread of Stepping

In searching for the reasons behind the spread of stepping to new venues, one cannot overlook the influence of the mass media, including film and television, as well as the Internet. The growing and widespread availability of home video equipment has contributed to the dissemination of stepping. Perhaps more important, the strong leadership and influence of black Greek alumni have also been instrumental in developing stepping in off-campus sites.

The first widespread exposure of stepping to the general public occurred in 1988 with *School Daze,* Spike Lee's film about African American college life. Lee uses a step show to replicate the tensions between Greeks and non-Greeks, a major theme of his work. The step show begins with Alpha Phi Alpha doing one of their signature chants, "Ice, Ice Baby" ("Ice, ice, baby, too cold, too cold. / Ice, ice, baby, the Black and Gold"). The Alpha steppers showcase a number of popular gymnastic-style steps such as "the Snake." For "the Snake," the brothers lie in a line on their bellies, one behind another with feet on each others' shoulders. The brother in front begins an undulating push-up that ripples slowly down the line. When the next group, the fictional Gamma Phi Gamma fraternity, steps, cracking begins and escalates the rivalry between the Gammas and a non-Greek faction led by Dap (Laurence Fishburne). In the audience, the female sweetheart organizations of both groups—the Gamma Rays and the Jigaboos—chant cracks at each other. The light-skinned Gamma Rays espouse white standards of beauty, whereas the darker-skinned Jigaboos reject Greek organizations and prefer African American standards. A non-Greek male group, "Da Fellas," heightens tensions by performing a step routine centered on insulting the Gammas. After calling them poor and fags, their crack step concludes with "get back, or we'll kick your Gamma ass." As Da Fellas exit the stage, a fight breaks out between them and the insulted Gammas.

School Daze brought the cultural politics of African American Greek-letter societies to the attention of a wider public, and stories about stepping began to appear in such widely read publications as *Rolling Stone* and the *Wall Street Journal.* The film *House Party II* contained stepping, as did certain episodes of television's *A Different World.* The first nationally syndicated stepping contest, *S.T.O.M.P* (Step Out National Championships), created by television producer and Kappa Alpha Psi member Frank Mercado-Valdes, aired in 1992. When Mercado-Valdes was creating the Miss Collegiate African

American Pageant in 1991 he saw a contestant perform a step routine for her talent competition. When he saw how that looked on the *Star Search* stage and how the audience responded to her talent, he recalled seeing other dynamic audience reactions at step shows. "Imagine," he exclaimed, "what they [the audience] would be doing if it was ten steppers." That led him to tape and syndicate a step show each year after the pageant. By 2000, Mercado-Valdes had produced seven shows that had been syndicated in ninety markets around the country, and he hoped to find a network slot for the program. In addition to *S.T.O.M.P.*, Mercado-Valdes and his partner Jimmy Hamilton have put together step shows for the Soul Train Music Awards, the NAACP Image Awards, and the American Television Awards.[3]

The mass media's impact on stepping should not be underestimated. After Alpha Phi Alpha from Howard University performed in a Footlocker commercial in December 1992, President-elect Bill Clinton's staff invited them to present four step shows at the inaugural festivities in 1993. A step team member attributed their invitation to the publicity gained from the commercial. Several students of the high school step team that began in 1995 in Blacksburg, Virginia, told me they wanted to step after seeing stepping on television, and the step coordinator of the Oak Grove African Methodist Episcopal Steppers in Detroit got some of her ideas from watching *S.T.O.M.P.* The opening ceremony of the 1996 Summer Olympics in Atlanta further propelled stepping into the limelight by featuring a team made up of members of black Greek-letter organizations. Contemporary gospel star Kirk Franklin included Christian stepping in his 1999 Nu Nation Tour, which featured the Steps of Praise Dancers. Widely circulated through pay-per-view television as well as on video, Franklin's tour reflected the popularity of Christian stepping and also stimulated its growth.[4]

Another strong influence on stepping's spread off-campus involves the widespread use of home video equipment. It is common to see several video cameras documenting any campus step show. These tapes circulate widely. Those who attend regional or national meetings of fraternities or sororities often videotape the step shows so they can show the newest steps to their brothers and sisters. Iota Phi Theta has produced a professional video about the fraternity that also contains excerpts from its step shows. Tyrone Petty says, laughing, that new groups have no need for his organizations to teach them how to do Christian stepping because "half the people had already videotaped us anyway." Web-sites make it possible for steppers to publicize shows and purchase step show videotapes.[5]

Because members of black Greek-letter organizations frequently assume leadership roles in the community, it is not surprising that they would use stepping as a vehicle for community improvement by teaching it to others. Conversely, people who have not attended college often find stepping attractive and ask fraternity and sorority members for help in learning. In 1992, for example, Cong. Maxine Waters organized a talent show among rival gang members at Nickerson Gardens, a housing project in South Central Los Angeles. The gang members, who had grown up in the same neighborhoods as Omega Psi Phi members and often attended fraternity step shows, asked Omega brothers to help them step for the talent show. The event helped achieve Waters's goal of building unity by providing a common ground, Omega member B'Jordan Brookins observes.[6]

The idea of using stepping to build unity is strong at the University of Texas at Austin, where Alpha Phi Alpha has promoted two events that encourage stepping among the entire student body. In their annual fall non-Greek step show, used to generate funds for scholarships, Alpha Phi Alpha sponsors a competitive event that gives other organizations an opportunity to step. Participants in the show, which began in 1988, include high school step teams, individual small groups, and second- and third-grade steppers from TRYBE (The Reason Young Blacks Excel). In a spring step show that takes place during the Alphas' Hope Week—organized to encourage "understanding and cooperation among different races and ethnic groups"— they teach representatives from a wide variety of campus organizations to step together. Twenty-five to thirty persons have stepped in the Hope Week show each year, among them blacks, whites, Hispanics, and Asians. Black Greek-letter organizations from around the country spread stepping among diverse groups in many ways as they seek to build bridges among people.[7]

Stepping in Religious Contexts

The church has always played a vital role in the spiritual and community life of many African Americans. Many churches have found that drill teams are a good way to keep youths active and teach them the scriptures. In the Church of God in Christ, the largest black Pentecostal denomination in the world with more than six million members, drill teams are an important component of youth ministry. Bishop Samuel L. Green, who presides over the Second Jurisdiction of Church of God in Christ, Virginia, said he thought of beginning church drill teams in 1977 because he was looking for something for young people to do. He remembers seeing drill teams in the House of Prayer for All People in Newport News when he was a young man, however, and thinks that the church might have had drill teams as early as the 1930s. Church drill

teams are now popular throughout the United States among COGIC church-
es, and they have become an important part of youth ministry among the
National Baptist denomination. In 1999 about sixty teams competed at the
National Baptist Convention of America in Tampa, Florida.[8]

The African American drill team tradition is similar to stepping in that
they both involve chanting and synchronized rhythm, although Christian
drill teams use a more regimented, militaristic style than Christian step teams.
The cadence tends to be a military four-beat, and marching commands such
as attention, parade rest, and left, right, and about-face orders are used. Team
members, their movements choreographed, recite Bible verses and the names
of the books of the Bible. A drill team rehearsal at Mt. Sinai Baptist Church
in Austin, Texas, is typical:

"Drill team!"

"Yes, sir!"

"Romans 10 and 17, recite!"

"So then faith cometh by hearing, and hearing by the word of God. Romans
10 and 17, siiirrr!"

"Don't give me lazy arms. You have to snap every move," said Leslie Dukes, a
Mt. Sinai drill team veteran who now serves as an assistant drill instructor.

Then he calls: "Drill team! Romans 10 and 17, recite!"

At the word "faith," team members put their right fists to their hearts.

At "cometh by hearing," they make a circular motion with their right hands
and then touch the tip of their ears. Their hands are straight and arms must be
rigidly angled from the body and parallel to the ground. At "by the word of God,"
their right hand fingers point to the 5-by-7-inch Bibles in their left hands, heads
bow toward the book and the right knee slightly bends with heel off the floor. All
three moves must occur simultaneously.

Finally, at "siiirrr!", all heads snap to the right.[9]

As stepping gained national attention during the late 1980s and early
1990s, drill teams began borrowing stepping styles. Javitta Wiley, co-cap-
tain of the Go Getters for Christ (GGFC) drill team at the Spirit of Life
Church of God in Christ in Farmville, Virginia, says that they begin and end
their show with traditional drill team moves but incorporate some stepping
into the middle. In the COGIC drill team competitions, each team has six
minutes to perform. Judges evaluate message, uniforms, facial expressions,
clarity, obedience to the drill sergeant, originality, and organization (coordination and synchronization).[10]

The intermingling of drill team and stepping traditions is complex. Although black drill teams likely played an important role in the emergence
of stepping among college fraternities and sororities, by the early 1990s

stepping had begun to influence drill team style. Three case studies stem directly from the influence of black Greek-letter societies on religious stepping rather than from the drill team tradition.

The Alpha Omega Alpha Christian Fellowship Fraternity, Inc.

> June 18, 1992, Prince George's County, Antioch Baptist Church, that was the day the Alpha Omega Alpha Christian Fellowship Fraternity was born. Directly, or indirectly, we have played a part in all of the step ministries that are here today. That's not a boast, that's only to say that God planted a seed and it's blooming. Because we have to stay fresh with our ministries to reach our young people. Amen? Amen. If you've ever worked with young people, you'll know what I'm talking about.

With these words, spoken at the "Christian Step Show and FUN-draiser," Tyrone Petty, credited his Christian fraternity for the spread of stepping ministries in the greater metropolitan area of Washington, D.C. Petty, in his thirties, radiates a spiritual light and energy. His masterful control of the "Christian Step Show and FUN-draiser," which I witnessed at the end of March 1997, drew me back to Washington in May to learn more about his stepping ministry. I talked with Petty and the fraternity co-leader, David Smith, who also emceed the Christian Step Show, about how and why they turned to stepping as a part of their ministry.[11]

In the spring of 1992, Petty, a youth minister at Antioch Baptist Church in Prince George's County was looking "for a way to involve all of our young people in our youth revival." Because he had many college-age and college students, he decided on a step show. On 17 and 18 June 1992 he organized young people at the revival into male and female step teams, and they performed. Because the participants wanted "to hold that together," Petty and four others—Joseph Sexton, John Scales, Michael Ware, and Antoine Powell—conceived of forming a Christian fraternity and sorority that would "be more than just stepping." They incorporated the Alpha Phi Alpha fraternity in November, 1992 and the Alpha Omega Delta sorority in 1993. Each of the founders had been involved with a variety of black fraternities in college, although Petty and his line at the University of the District of Columbia never "crossed over" into Alpha Phi Alpha. In designing the new Christian fraternity, they "brought together every component" they could think of, such as "the brothers and the sisters and evangelism, pledging, the discipleship, the development, and the outreach."[12]

Joining the fraternity or sorority involves a two-stage process of "discipling," by which Petty means "building a concrete understanding for young Christians" and preparing for "hard-core evangelism," which takes them "into the street, to the neighborhoods where most folks won't go." In 1999 thirty-six brothers were in the fraternity, and thirty-five to forty sisters had joined the sorority. Their average age was nineteen, although the youngest member pledged at fifteen and the oldest was around forty-three. In 1997 the fraternity and the sorority began organizing youth divisions at St. Paul Baptist Church and the Antioch Baptist Church, and by 1999 they had organized two coeducational divisions for ages twelve to eighteen. The youth divisions also step and focus on discipleship and outreach.[13]

Because the founders had been involved with college fraternities, it was natural for them to incorporate stepping into the new organization. The "major difference between us and secular fraternities," David Smith stresses, is that "our bottom line is ministry. And if we're not doing ministry, we're not doing it." Consequently, their Christian stepping differs from secular stepping. Instead of stepping to display unity, Smith says, "our stepping is mainly ministry and we don't step to display ourselves. Our stepping is just a tool to share our message. Every step that we do has an evangelistic thrust behind it, and if it doesn't, we don't do it."[14]

Stepping is a vital component—"the glue," as Smith terms it—of their outreach ministry. Putting it another way, Petty observes, "If we didn't have the stepping it would become mundane, but if all we had was the stepping, it would become fruitless." Once, Smith recalls, five or six members of the fraternity were at Iverson Mall in Hillcrest Heights, Maryland, and had spent several hours "walking around, passing out flyers and talking to people, and showing them passages of scripture and praying with folks." Although he would not say they "were unsuccessful," Smith reports that everything changed when his cousin saw them and asked them to step. "And before we knew it, moments, the mall was packed." The "mall stopped" says Smith. Petty adds, "The people were warm. . . . And it just opened all kinds of barriers. We were able to witness to people. People were receptive." Even the security guard who "stood on the steps and waited till we were finished, came over to us and said, 'I'm supposed to tell you that you cannot do that here. I've told you.' He turned and walked away, as if to say, 'You all do your thing, do what you have to do.'"[15]

Interest in Alpha Omega Alpha began to grow in August 1992, when they stepped in a youth revival and then at a concert by gospel singer John P. Kee, where they "broke loose." After that appearance, the fraternity "got invitations from everywhere," but in those early days the "pastors were being careful about inviting us." Although some might resist the idea of stepping in church as undignified or disrespectful, Petty remarks, they do not try to confront them but rather respect their beliefs and realize that stepping "is not a tool that is easily acceptable because some people have had bad experiences with fraternities and sororities." People often want "to see us in presentation before we are invited to their churches," says Petty.[16]

The springboard for the group was its first appearance in evangelist Marsha Sumner's first Holy Ghost Throw Down in 1992. Sumner began her interdenominational youth ministry by sponsoring such events, when young people minister to other young people by sharing their talents in vocal and instrumental solos, choirs, and reading the scriptures. She invited Tyrone Petty and his Christian fraternity to step in her first Throw Down, and they have stepped in each of them since.[17]

Although Alpha Omega Alpha focuses on leading people to Christ, Petty explains that they are not a church and do not perform all church rituals. They always have a praise circle (praise and prayer) before and after stepping. Sometimes they have been invited to church services in lieu of formal preaching, and in some situations they have opened "the door to the church, to the altar call." In a street setting, "If we're out there evangelizing and someone does come to Christ, at that moment we converge and pray right there, but then we try to help that person find a church home."[18]

The AAMEN Steppers

When fifteen smartly dressed young boys marched onto stage at the "Christian Step Show and FUN-draiser" in Washington, D.C., in March 1997, the crowd stood and cheered. The youngest steppers that day, the boys ranged between first and fourth grade. Dressed alike in black pants, long-sleeved white shirts, and bow ties and suspenders, they excelled in precise, intricately patterned movement. Their adaptation of the "Centaur Walk" step revealed the strong influence of Iota Phi Theta fraternity.

Their step coordinator, Quentin Hudgens, is a member of the Beta Omega graduate chapter, Polaris, of Iota Phi Theta. His chapter organized the African-American Male Educational Network as a mentoring project at St. Francis Xavier School, South East, in Washington in 1993. Two or three times a week, Hudgens leaves his job as a computer specialist at Ft. Meade, Maryland, and, along with another brother, becomes an after-school mentor to twenty-five young boys who range in age from eight to thirteen. The Iota Phi Theta brothers tutor the boys in "academic, social, and leadership skills" along with stepping as a recreational activity. In order to participate on the step team, the children must establish and maintain a 3.0 grade average. The originator of the group, Ed Rubin, a graduate of Rutgers University, taught the boys nearly twenty step routines before he moved to St. Louis. Hudgens and the group work on perfecting the routines and devising variations on them. When I talked with him in May 1997, he had been working with the boys for three or four months.[19]

Hudgens said he has seen definite growth in discipline among the children as a result of participation in stepping: "If you want to do good and perform well, it takes discipline, and it takes hard work and it takes commitment. People always compliment them on how very well-behaved they are, and I think that comes from just the discipline that we have had to instill. Because we are working with twenty-five boys, and that can get tight sometimes."[20]

The AAMEN Steppers have performed in a variety of settings, including at churches, schools, and the Department of Housing and Urban Development, as well as for the American Heart Association and around the nation. The group is only one example of the Iota National Youth Alliance, "a national umbrella program through which individual chapters of Iota Phi Theta address the needs of Black Youth in their communities." The AAMEN initiative in Washington, D.C., has made a difference in the academic performance of the young people who participate in it. "The forty young men currently enrolled in the program are collectively in the top 5 percent of their classes."[21]

The Oak Grove Steppers

In 1994 the Rev. Jessica Ingram, assistant minister of the Oak Grove African Methodist Episcopal Church in Detroit, Michigan, asked member Ilyasah Nikkia Upshaw to start a step team for the church's young people. By 1996 forty-five youths, aged six to eighteen, were performing once a month during the service. The *Detroit News* featured the team, which also performed at an international gathering of A.M.E. churches, the Thirteenth Quadrennial Convention of the Young People's Division in Detroit. Although Ingram has been a Delta soror since the late 1960s and was one of the first members of Delta Sigma Theta sorority at the University of Missouri, that group did not do the complicated stepping done now. When she graduated in 1969, stepping on the Missouri campus involved marching on line and singing. Ingram describes herself as being unfamiliar with step shows, and although friends at A.M.E. churches in Maryland and New York had started step teams she had never seen those groups perform. Her decision to begin a step team, Ingram said, "grew out of a concern that I had for the young people of our church and them needing to have something that required discipline, but also promoted praising God and I know that young people like movement and dance and rhythm, so to speak, and I wanted them to engage in something that was positive." Ingram's motiva-

tion is similar to that of Christopher Hill, the youth pastor at New Cove-
nant Christian Center in Mattapan, Massachusetts, who helped establish
the Alpha and Omega Steppers at the church: "We strive to reach the next
generation and will use any Godly means we can find."[22]

The first step coordinator of the Oak Grove Steppers, Nikkia Upshaw, is
a graduate of Wayne State University but did not pledge a sorority. She did,
however, attend fraternity and sorority events where stepping was done and
was in a little sisters organization of the AKAs while in high school. The
stepping style of Omega Psi Phi, which she believes is masculine and powerful, has influenced her choreography. Her experience with cheerleading
and in gymnastics, coupled with seeing many step shows, prepared her to
coordinate the Oak Grove Steppers. When asked how she makes up words
to steps, she replied:

> It might sound a bit bizarre, but I pray. I prayed on them. This is something that
> we honestly feel . . . was a divine order of things. To take something that was total-
> ly secular and transform everything back to God. You know we are under the be-
> lief that everything is for the good of God. And anything that is out in the world
> was once good, even if it's been turned bad, it was once good. And with that belief,
> before I do anything with the kids, I pray on it. Because we look at it as a worship
> experience. It's a different way of worship, but it also connects the kids with their
> own personal relationship with their savior. So I prayed on the words.[23]

Several steps that the Oak Grove Steppers perform define stepping in
church as a religious practice. For their first performance, they said:

> (*Audience responses are in italics.*)
> Can you hear, hear, hear, hear,
> *Uh huh.*
> all the beat, beat, beat, beat?
> *That's right.*
> We praise the Lord, Lord, Lord, Lord,
> *Yes.*
> with our feet, feet, feet, feet.
> Now ain't that sweet?
> *Yeah, yeah.*
> (*Wordless stepping continues.*)

In another step from the same performance they continued:

> O.G.S. is right on time,
> *Uh huh.*
> praising God with steps and rhyme.
> *Uh huh, yeah.*[24]

Like many college groups, the Oak Grove Steppers claim that stepping originated in Africa: "Africa is where stepping began, / from the beat of the drums to the sound of our feet / using rhythms and rhymes / singing praises unto thee."[25]

In the introduction to their first church step show on 30 November 1994 they said, "Greetings in the name of our Father, who was both Alpha and Omega. We bring you greetings from O.G.S., on a mission representing the youth ministry." After their performance, the youth minister, the Rev. Mark Thomas, praised the steppers and said to the congregation, "But being a gentleman, you know that they stole most of those steps from my fraternity, most noble lords of the upper house, Alpha Phi Alpha fraternity, Incorporated. But not the Kappas. We thank God anyhow. Amen. You see they're stepping for Jesus, and you ain't got to worry about the Greek-letter fraternal organizations. Is that right? We ain't whippin' on them, amen? A-men." (Echoing the style and content of Alpha Phi Alpha's trade step "The Grand-daddy," the team changed its words to praise God at another church service.)[26]

The congregation reacted enthusiastically to their first step show but not without some criticism. "It was the most crowded I had ever seen our church. We couldn't get everyone in. It was phenomenal," recalls Upshaw. "The reaction at first I thought would be really mixed, but it was like an overwhelming, overnight success. I mean everyone was up off the pews. I mean you would not have thought this was church. One very old lady said, 'These children shouldn't be stomping around in the congregation,' but then she turned right back around and said, 'but if it keeps them in church, then it's OK.'"[27]

Ingram knows that the entertainment value of stepping has the potential to distract the Oak Grove Steppers from their main mission, praising God. Consequently, even though the group receives frequent invitations to step outside the church, "We have really restricted those because we did not want them to get it in their heads that they are entertaining or that they begin to think of themselves too highly."[28]

The Blacksburg High School Black Awareness Club Steppers

In contrast to the Oak Grove A.M.E. Church, where stepping started at the desire of an adult who had pledged a sorority, at the predominantly white Blacksburg High School in Blacksburg, Virginia, students in the Black Awareness Club became interested in stepping after seeing it performed on television and at Virginia Tech. In 1993, three years before the club started stepping, the group's leader Tameka Gumbs and some friends learned to step by videotaping steppers at Virginia Tech, imitating them, and changing their words. When the club decided to step, Gumbs asked the president of the Eta Lambda chapter of Omega Psi Phi, Tamer Mokhtar, and Vincent Jones for help. The club's first performance, before the entire school on 28 February 1996, showed the Omega imprint. One tune, used in many Omega steps, is sung in a minor key, like a spiritual: "All of my love, my peace and happiness, I'm gonna give it to Omega" (fig. 43). In the high school version, the steppers sang the same tune and the words, "All of my love, my peace and happiness, I'm gonna give it to my people."[29]

Figure 43. "All of My Love" as sung by Omega Psi Phi fraternity, Virginia Tech, 1995.

The Omegas were not the only influence on the Blacksburg High School Steppers, however. Tameka Gumbs and her fellow steppers composed their entrance step, which they call the "Mary J. Blige Step," to the song "Real Love." Gumbs copied the step from high school students who performed in front of the bleachers at a step show at the Agricultural and Technical State University in Greensboro, North Carolina.[30]

The Blacksburg High School administration was at first apprehensive about allowing a schoolwide assembly for a step show. They worried about whether the performance would hold the attention of the audience and be educational. To answer that concern, the Omegas wrote a skit that involved the steppers and also professors from Virginia Tech who talked about the history of stepping and other African American traditions. The skit and step show were performed during Black History Month as a way of teaching African American history. Audience response was enthusiastic, and numerous students expressed interest in stepping the following year.

When asked how stepping has changed her, Tameka Gumbs replied, "I take things much more seriously. Stepping has taught me that if I commit to something, I have to commit all the way. It has taught me to have patience, if I can't learn a step. It has taught me to pay attention."[31]

The Gamma Beta Tau Step Club

We are the steppers
from Trimble Tech.
You too can make a difference
in your community.

We step with pride
and not for show.
We step with unity
wherever we go.

To these words of their signature step, the Gamma Beta Tau Step Club of Forth Worth, Texas, proudly marches onstage. Sporting a tough, military look, the male team in 1998–99 wore green and black camouflage pants, black shirts, green camouflage bandannas on their heads, and large, green-painted "stomping boots." The female team wore white painters' overalls, on the left leg of which was a picture of a female bulldog performing a step (the school mascot is a bulldog). On the right leg were the letters *GBT.* The bib itself sported the Greek letters *gamma, beta,* and *tau.*[32]

The first high school step team in Fort Worth, Gamma Beta Tau began in the fall of 1994 when two students, Bertha Joshua and LaCandra Thomas, asked mathematics teacher Sadie E. Allen to sponsor a step club at Green B. Trimble Technical High School. At first she turned them down; she "had never heard of a high school group stepping." Although she had been a member of Alpha Kappa Alpha in 1970 at the University of North Texas at Denton, she recalls her sorority as "too ladylike" to step in those days. Instead, they sang, serenaded, and "did little cutesy dance routines in heels and dresses."

The students prevailed, however, and Allen sponsored the step club, which traveled with the school recruitment team to middle schools during its first year. "After that, word just sort of spread and everybody else started doing it [stepping]. And I thought, well maybe this isn't so bad after all," Allen notes. Now, stepping is "one of [my] favorite subjects." The GBT Step Club performs in at least two step shows in the fall and anywhere from four to eight shows in the spring. Stepping is "so hot" that the Trimble school fund-raiser has shifted from candy sales to an annual step show, one of which raised $1,200 for scholarships to pay for college textbooks.

Green B. Trimble Technical High School, predominantly black, is located in a tough area close to downtown Fort Worth, and nearly 40 percent of its students are Latino. It is not in a residential neighborhood, but it is close to homeless shelters, a hospital, and mental health services. Students at

Trimble come from throughout the Fort Worth School District if they are interested in learning trades.

The step team began with about thirty students; most were female although the group was coeducational. Many members had performance experience in church drill teams or choirs. As the popularity of stepping has grown in Fort Worth, Dallas, and throughout the country, the club's membership has increased. In 1998–99 Allen had to bar freshmen from participating, and she split the club into male and female teams. The 1998–99 step club had an eighteen-member male team and a female team of about twenty-five. Two were white.

Oral tradition plays a big role in the process of composing new steps, and college stepping strongly influences the Gamma Beta Tau steppers. "The kids are constantly going to area colleges, to Greek shows, and if they have cousins that are at different colleges, they find out from them what's going on," says Allen. "They come home for holidays and they teach them steps so they can bring them back to the group." Allen refers to this borrowing process as "stealing": "We steal whatever we can. And we try to steal it first, so that when we do go to a step show, people are stealing from us. We pride ourselves in being the first to do something." The borrowing process involves creative adaptations. At one event, the Alphas used a fog machine and entered from a refrigerator-like structure, saying, "'Oooh, it's cold in here, must be some Alphas in the atmosphere.'" The Gamma Beta Tau steppers copied that idea by emerging from a small doghouse, also on a fog-filled stage. "Oooh," they said. "You just can't see through the fog, it must be the trail of a (x) Gamma Dog." (The x indicates a missing downbeat.)

Although Allen had no experience stepping, she had seen stepping by fraternities when she was in college. She had also watched it on television and had seen her son, who pledged Alpha Phi Alpha in 1992, step. She does not step with the club but tells them "what I like and what I don't like," or, perhaps, "There's a beat missing there, or there's something that needs to be put there." "Every last one" of her students say they want to join a fraternity or sorority when they go to college. "All the girls want to be AKAs and all the boys want to be Alphas," Allen says. "The boys are A Phi A crazy, you know, the ice. They're so hot and they're so cold. They call themselves the sons of fire and ice."

Participating in the Gamma Beta Tau Step Club has brought positive changes to students. Just as the state of Texas's University Interscholastic League enforces a "no pass, no play" rule in sports, Allen has developed her own standards: "no pass, no step." Students who fail a class or are insubordinate are not allowed to step. As Allen says, "When we start bringing home trophies [then it's] cool to step, everybody wants to step, nobody wants to get kicked off for any reason. So it has improved their behavior. It has improved their ability to work with others, and it has improved their academic status also."

The group usually rehearses for an hour after school on Tuesday, Wednesday, and Thursday afternoons and for longer periods if a show approaches. Step shows in the Fort Worth–Dallas area fall into two categories: noncompetitive showcases and competitive "step-offs" for trophies and or money. The undergraduate chapter of Kappa Alpha Psi fraternity at the University of Texas at Arlington began sponsoring high school step-offs in 1997–98, and by 1999 the Trimble steppers had won two seconds and a third in that competition. They also won two first places in the Grand Prairie High School step show in 1997–98 and a third-place trophy and $50 at Martin High School's first step show in Arlington in 1999.

Gamma Beta Tau has grown in numbers and in status. At one recent homecoming, in addition to asking former cheerleaders and drill team members to come forward, organizers "asked for the old steppers to come up and do a little something." One of the best step club captains "comes back all the time," Allen notes. "It started out being an alternative group and now . . . whenever the principal has to showcase what's going on at the school, she takes my group. You know, it's gotten a lot more mainstream than it was."

Latino Greek-letter Organization Stepping

When the eight members of Lambda Upsilon Lambda Fraternity marched onto the gym floor at Roberto Clemente State Park in the Bronx in the summer of 1999, they wore the brown fatigues and sweatshirts ("gold hoodies") that the line pledging the Caballeros (their pledge club) wear during a calculated stage in their pledge process. Moving so closely together in their "line march" that their bodies touched, the group quickly shed the hoodies to reveal shiny gold sportshirts emblazoned with the word *Lambda* on the fronts and a large brown 82 (the year of their founding at Cornell University) on the backs. Before they finished, the brothers had shed the gold shirts as well and stepped in sleeveless undershirts.

Over the course of their show, the brothers of Lambda Upsilon Lambda enacted the social drama of pledging, the unity of their brotherhood, and their competition with other fraternities as they humorously cracked on other Latino fraternities in a skit. "Oooh I feel it! Oooh I feel it! Oooh I feel it!" they chanted to build suspense before their second routine, which began with a chant that envisioned the thirteen founders ("knights") of the fraternity taking the hands of the pledges and telling them they are special:

I looked to the sky
and what did I see?
I saw the thirteen knights
looking down at me.
They took my hand
and said "understand
you're a brother
like no other.
You're a Lambda man."
Oooh![33]

On the word *oooh*, the brothers froze into a sitting position, one leg crossed and resting on a knee, elbows resting on the elevated knee, and chins resting on folded hands. Because the steppers were standing, they had to mime a position of repose while balancing on one leg (fig. 42). The pose embodies the up-scale, Ivy League image that Lambda brothers esteem. When they exited in another line march, each brother grasped the chest of the person in front. The group then rocked from side to side, seeming to be a single multilegged organism (fig. 44).

Figure 44. Brothers of Lambda Upsilon Lambda fraternity exit in a "line walk" that demonstrates their unity. Latino-Greek Step and Stroll Show, 1999. (Photograph and video by Hazen Robert Walker)

African American fraternities and sororities have been stepping for at least fifty years, possibly more, but stepping is a very new ritual performance among a rapidly expanding number of Latino Greek fraternities and sororities. The first intercollegiate Latino Greek step and stroll show on the East Coast, and perhaps in the nation, took place at the Roberto Clemente State Park in the Bronx on 24 July 1999. Intercollegiate step and stroll teams from seven Latino sororities and three fraternities performed to an overflow crowd in the gymnasium. The heat index was 110 that summer day in the Bronx, but the enthusiastic crowd of around eight hundred stayed for four hours to watch the noncompetitive show organized by Anthony Aldaño and Nada Bahbahani. Four Latino Greek organizations that did not step in the show turned out in numbers to offer support.

Like African American students, Latino students organized Greek-letter societies to support and unite those who are a minority at predominantly white institutions. The oldest Latino Greek organization, Phi Iota Alpha, Inc. (also known by a Spanish transliteration as Fi Iota Alfa), formed at Rensselaer Polytechnic Institute in 1931 from the merger of two earlier Latino Greek-letter societies. The first, La Unión Hispano Americana (UHA), founded in 1898 at Rensselaer, became Fi Lamda Alfa in 1921 after merging with Pi Delta Fi and Fi Lamda Alfa. In 1931 Fi Lamda Alfa merged with Sigma Iota (founded as Sociedad Hispano-Americana at Louisiana State University in 1904) to become Fi Iota Alfa. Due to a drastic loss of Latino enrollment at U.S. universities during World War II and through 1952, the chapters of Fi Iota Alfa sharply declined. By 1968 only Rensselaer's was active, but that, too, closed in 1973. In 1984, however, a new chapter of Fi Iota Alfa started at Rensselaer helped by Fi Iota Alfa brothers. By 1999 it had fourteen undergraduate chapters and four alumni chapters throughout the northeastern United States. During the 1980s, fourteen Latino Greek societies organized, and by the mid-1990s twenty-one more had begun. By 1999 there were twenty-five Latino sororities, thirteen fraternities, and one coeducational Greek organization.[34]

These Latino-based organizations are multicultural and attract not only a diverse Latino population encompassing persons with African, mestizo, and European ancestry but also non-Latino Caucasians and those who have Middle-Eastern and Asian ancestries. That diversity was well-represented at the 1999 show.

Nada Bahbahani, co-founder of the Delta chapter of Lambda Pi Upsilon sorority, Latinas Poderosas Unidas, Inc., at Columbia University in 1996, is the daughter of immigrants from Iraq. Because she grew up in New York City and has many Latino friends, and because she sees great similarities in Latino and Middle Eastern cultures, she chose to join a Latino sorority. "I'm not Latina," she acknowledges, "but I feel a connection. I feel like we all have a similarity in what we strive for and our goals. We strive to help the community and to help the disadvantaged. Women, number one, and those of color, number two."[35] One other Middle Eastern woman, of Lebanese descent, is also in the sorority.

When she was in high school, Bahbahani shared the popular stereotype that college fraternities and sororities only drink and party, and she "wasn't interested in going to parties and drinking. I was more interested in activism." She "wanted to work with others with similar goals to make a difference," believing that "with numbers, you can get further in helping the community." Establishing a sisterhood added "an extra plus." Like many Latino Greek organizations, Lambda Pi Upsilon is young. It started in 1992 at SUNY, Geneseo and as of 2002 had six chapters and two colonies. The sorority is active in big sister–little sister mentoring programs and also raises money for women's shelters.[36]

Stepping is new to Lambda Pi Upsilon. Bahbahani stepped for the first time in 1997 as part of Latino Heritage Month at Columbia University. She and her seven sisters from several colleges and universities in the New York area learned to step from being exposed to Greek stepping and from the help of a sister who choreographs. Because the sorority has not been stepping long, it has not developed trade or signature steps. Most steps they did in the Roberto Clemente State Park show were nonverbal, but in the first step after their entrance they accompanied themselves with a chant:

Hey all my sisters
strong and united gather around
so we can show them
what it means to be a Lambda Pi Upsilon.
My sisters. . . . Let's show them how it goes.
In '92, we started representing the Red, White, Gold, and Black.
Taking it back to our roots,
our six founding mothers
together as one,
the inspiration for
Latinas Poderosas Unidas.
We are the proof that
together as one,
con amor, dignidad, y orgullo (with love, dignity, and pride),
we sought the Lambda way
and continued the legacy.

Hermanas para siempre! (Sisters forever!)[37]

The selective use of Spanish words is one way the sorority expresses pride in Hispanic culture. Although the words conveyed Latino identity, the stepping differed little in style from that of black Greeks. In contrast, the Latino groups performed their strolls or party walks to popular Latino music and with many Latino dance movements from the salsa, rumba, and marengue.

Although Lambda Upsilon Lambda (La Unidad Latina) fraternity, to which Anthony Aldaño belongs, is ten years older than Lambda Pi Upsilon sorority, it, too, is relatively new to stepping. Founded at Cornell University in 1982, LUL <http://www.launidadlatina.org> has chapters at seven of the eight Ivy League schools and forty-one chapters on the East Coast. Service activities range from voter registration drives to raising money for victims of Hurricane Mitch, which ravaged several Central American countries in 1998.[38]

Aldaño became interested in stepping while attending Johnson and Wales University in Providence, Rhode Island, in the early 1990s. He was attracted by the "show aspect" of stepping, which he describes as "very fun, soulful, and proud." Aldaño, who is of Peruvian and Dominican Republic ancestry, pledged at Brown University in 1994, and his fraternity stepped with black fraternities during homecoming at Duke University in 1996. After he graduated in 1997, he became active in the graduate chapter.[39]

The eight brothers, five graduates and three undergraduates, on the intercollegiate team that Aldaño formed for the step show responded to an e-mail announcement. They came from eight universities and rehearsed for four months, once a week at first and building to three or four times a week, for up to three or four hours a session. Such intensive rehearsals demanded commitment. For Aldaño, it meant giving up his Saturday mornings and commuting into New York City from his home in New Jersey.[40]

Several factors help explain stepping's appeal to Latino youths. Many participants in the Roberto Clemente State Park show were from the Bronx and the New York City area, birthplace of hip-hop culture, and those who enjoy hip-hop also enjoy the rapping chants of stepping. Many, too, although from a Spanish-speaking heritage such as those of the Dominican Republic, Cuba, or Puerto Rico, are also of African heritage. The powerful African aesthetic that permeates stepping presents a familiar movement and performance context. Both Latino and African-based rhythms have mixed for more than half a century in Latin music from New York City, as Steven Loza argues in *Tito Puente and the Making of Latin Music*. During the Palladium Ballroom era in the late 1940s through the 1950s, that club, located on Broadway, "became a multicultural forum for what might now be called performance art." Tito Puente has recalled that the Palladium "was a big melting pot—Jews, Italians, Irish, Blacks, Puerto Ricans, Cubans, you name it. Everyone was equal under the roof of the Palladium because everyone was there to dig the music and to dance." Borrowing a comment made by Max Salazar, Loza argues that "the Palladium and its Latin music did more for integration than all the theories and methods of social scientists. Music, dance and the art of it all seemed to captivate the soul, exorcising the physical and cultural restrictions of a historically segregated society."[41]

Before the reemergence of Latino Greek-letter organizations in the 1980s, Latino students would often join African American fraternities and sororities. One of Kappa Alpha Psi's well-known brothers, Arturo Alfonso Schomburg, who pledged the Omicron chapter around 1922 and "later helped to organize the New York Alumni Chapter," was "a Puerto Rican of African descent." Schomburg "identified himself with black people and the Harlem Renaissance" and dedicated his life to collecting "books, art pieces and other evidences from around the world to prove that 'the Negro had a long and honorable past.'" His collection, now known as the Schomburg Center for Research in Black Culture, is housed at the New York Public Library. William L. Crump calls the Schomburg Center a tribute to the leadership of Kappa Alpha Psi.[42]

Just as the NAACP in 1999 announced a new goal of reaching out to Latinos in order to build a power base for people of color, black and Latino Greek organizations are beginning to work together on college campuses. In 1998, for example, the Black Greek Council at West Chester University (WCU) in Pennsylvania changed its name. It is now the Black and Latino Greek Council (BLGC), a change that shows "the council's commitment to be progressive in a changing diverse collegiate community." The BLGC "strives to promote unity and cooperation amongst the minority Greeks on WCU's campus."[43] With this close affiliation, sharing the popular movement tradition of stepping seems natural.

The success of the first Latino Step and Stroll Show has led to an annual Latino step show as well as to a Web-site, <http://www.LatinosStep.Com>. Developed by Anthony Aldaño and Jesus Diaz, Jr., in 2001, the site features pictures and video clips of Latino step teams as well as educational material about Latino culture and stepping.

Asian Greek-letter Organization Stepping

Like Latino Greek-Letter organizations, some Asian fraternities and sororities also step. Some chapters began in the early 1990s, others in 1998. The producer of *S.T.O.M.P.*, Frank Mercado-Valdes, recalls a northern California Asian fraternity that sent him a tape in 1993 "that just did stepping."

Although he was unable to remember the organization's name or school, Mercado-Valdes describes the team as "incredible" and "phenomenal." He "was tempted to put them on, and then thought the backlash may be so severe from the black fraternities and sororities that it would be too much of a risk for a one-time-only situation."[44] In 1993 *S.T.O.M.P.* focused on the stepping of black Greek-letter organizations in the National Pan-Hellenic Council. Consequently, the producers excluded not only the Asian team but also high school teams.

Although some black Greeks feel that stepping belongs to them and do not want Greeks who are not black to step, others, such as the Alpha Phi Alpha fraternity at the University of Texas at Austin, use stepping as a way of building unity among various organizations, including an Asian-interest sorority, Sigma Phi Omega.[45]

Four sisters of Sigma Phi Omega learned to step during the 1998 Alpha Phi Alpha–sponsored Hope Week step show, so their stepping style resembles that of the Alphas says Trang Nguyen. Although they have not developed chants, the steps they use have some of the same rhythms as the Alphas'. During rush, Nguyen notes, "We do skits and dances and we have stepping in our dances." She is "not really sure" that her group will continue stepping, because it is "a lot harder than it looks." Members of an Indian sorority, Kappa Phi Gamma, participated in the Project Hope Week step show in 1999.[46]

At the University of Michigan, the first South Asian interest fraternity, Alpha Iota Omicron, has begun to shape and express its cultural identity through stepping. Founded on 16 October 1998, the organization performed its first step show in October 2000 at the Indian American Student Association Cultural Show in Ann Arbor and its second show, on 23 March 2001, was at the Generation APA show, a pan-Asian cultural event. Co-founder and stepmaster Nihar Kulkarni, whose parents are natives of Belgaum in the Indian state of Maharashtra, learned to step from a close friend in Phi Beta Sigma fraternity, Marcus Collins. After their first step show, which closely resembled African American stepping, Kulkarni began to add rhythms and movements from traditional South Asian dances, such as the *raas* and *garba* from the Gujarat state of India and *bhangra* music from the Punjab region, to provide a rhythmic base. Alpha Iota Omicron's stepping style is still being developed, Kulkarni says. They are working on core steps that will express cultural identity and eternal brotherhood. Kulkarni observes that the fraternity finds stepping useful in building unity between brothers. Through the discipline required to work together and synchronize movements, the brothers build a strong group identity. Kulkarni hopes they will be able to combine traditional stepping with their own cultural identity.[47]

Step Afrika! An International Arts Organization

In their week of appearances at the Kennedy Center during January 2000, the international arts organization Step Afrika! presented a stunning performance of South African and African American dance traditions, including stepping. The South African branch of Step Afrika!—the Soweto Dance Theatre—performed a gumboot dance and two contemporary dance selections. The first, "For the Soul," was a "dance of initiation of a church-going person into an Umngoma (a traditional healer)"; "Still My Friend" was a dance of "friendship, jealousy, neglect, acceptance, and celebrations." Joining with the members of Step Afrika! USA, they performed "Party Walk" and "The Zulu Dance—Finale." The American members of Step Afrika! featured Greek-letter society stepping in two numbers. In "For the Brothers," they performed "the male tradition of stepping as preserved by brothers of the Alpha Phi Alpha Fraternity, Inc." "High Steppin' Sorors" was "the female tradition of stepping as expressed by sisters of Delta Sigma Theta Sorority, Inc."[48]

One of the most powerful dances, "Wade in the Water," brilliantly combined South African gumboot dancing, tap dancing, and African American stepping. A collaborative effort choreographed by Paul Woodruff, Kirsten Smith, and LeeAnet Noble, the dance began with dancer Paul Woodruff and two singers coming onstage in choir robes and singing the spiritual "Wade in the Water." Walking forward from the choir to center-stage, Woodruff sat in a straight-backed chair and slowly began to put on knee-high gumboots while the chorus continued singing. Standing, he started a powerful gumboot dance, creating percussive sounds by slapping the boots and stomping. As the tune and lyrics shifted to "take me to the water to be baptized," LeeAnet Noble, dressed in a long white baptismal gown, was led onstage by a man carrying a Bible. She began a tap dance that rhythmically interplayed with the sounds of the gumboot dance. Entering on Woodruff's left, Kirsten Smith began an African American stepping routine. As the music continued, the three rhythmic traditions united in a rich, polyrhythmic fugue.

After the two shows of the day, the directors and dancers of Step Afrika! gathered in the Kennedy Center's atrium to give at least two hundred children and adults a workshop that included some South African gumboot and Zulu dance moves and a short African American stepping routine (fig. 41). For the first time since Step Afrika! was founded in 1994, its South African branch was performing in the United States. The story of the founding of this international arts organization illustrates not only the attraction of stepping to other cultures but also stepping's ability to open doors to better intercultural communication.

The nucleus of the idea for Step Afrika! began in 1991 when Brian Williams, a Howard graduate and a member of Alpha Phi Alpha fraternity, was working in Lesotho, Africa, teaching business skills at a vocational school. While driving down a street one day, he saw a young boy doing a dance:

> When I first saw it . . . I remember it clearly . . . and I just turned my head like, "what in the world," because it looked like he was doing stepping. And it wasn't just the movement, but it was the spirit. Like I said, he was doing it by himself, it might be like a frat brother on the corner just getting excited and just doing Alpha kicks. So that's how we feel about it sometimes. You might be just hanging out with your friends and just start stepping. Because its one way that you express yourself when you're happy. . . . And I was fresh out of my collegiate experience. . . . I had been in many step shows and worked hard on step shows. So I was very intrigued by it.[49]

When Williams returned to class and asked his students about the dance he had seen on the street, they identified it as a gumboot dance and showed him some steps. Williams asked if they had ever seen stepping, and because they had not he "explained a little a bit about what it was" and then "showed them some steps." Amazed at what they saw, the African students did a "mini-exchange" of dances with Williams at his Lesotho apartment. Williams found that this exchange of dance traditions improved their communication:

> We were dancing together, and I liked the spirit that was brought about in our communication. I think . . . when I first arrived in Lesotho, a lot of them didn't understand why I identified so much with the continent of Africa. Because I looked totally different. African Americans, of course, look different at this point, different colors, different hair textures and what not from most South Africans who are born there. And they may not have understood why I was so enthusiastic and why I called myself African American. After that, they were able to understand me a little bit better, we were able to communicate better, and I thought that . . . the sharing of dance traditions, especially the sharing of traditional and social dance, was an excellent way to break down barriers between cultures and open up the lines for dialogue.[50]

After his fellowship ended in 1992, Williams flew back to the United States. En route, he began to write down what he wanted to do when he got back. As he reviewed his options, teaching or working with an international organization, the "one thing" he wrote down "was Step Afrika!" but "that was just an idea." Williams went to work in the South African Programs Department of Africare for three years, a job that took him back to Johannesburg in January 1994. There he saw the Soweto Dance Theatre perform at the Civic Theatre in Johannesburg, where he met Mbuyiselwa Jackie Semela, the founding director, and Thembinkosi Hlatshawayo, a dancer for the company who is now its managing director. Semela and Hlatshawayo took Williams to Soweto and showed him their dance programming for the township. They showed him the gumboot and Zulu dance. Williams in return showed them "some steps," and "they had the same response as those young brothers in Lesotho. . . . They were like, 'Wow, this is so similar. How is that, how do you do this, how did we not know about it? Let's do something about this.' And I told them about my idea. And they said, 'We should do a festival here in South Africa that would bring the two dance forms together. And then maybe we might find some ideas as to how it all started or how two different art forms could be done on different continents by people who are different, but also very much the same.'"[51]

Williams, Hlatshawayo, and another dancer from Soweto Dance Theatre, Moeketsi Koena, began working every night "to structure a festival that would bring the two art forms together, but would also expose the Americans that [he] would bring to the continent to the other traditions within South Africa." They planned the Step Afrika! International Cultural Festival, in which "the Americans and South Africans would share their dance traditions with the young children from the township." The festival "offer[ed] daily workshops over a period of two weeks—culminating in a series of African dance performances by international and local dance companies and artists and a colourful street carnival."[52]

Williams returned to America in March of 1994 and introduced the idea of the Step Afrika! festival to his fraternity brothers at Howard. In the next months they raised $15,000 so twelve members of the fraternity, along with two women, could return to South Africa in December and participate. In 1995 Williams brought another U.S. delegation to the Step Afrika! festival, and that same year a dance troupe came from London. The London delegation, headed by choreographers Khadijatu Frasier and H. Patten, organized Step Afrika! U.K. It shares U.K. urban dance styles along with numerous Caribbean dance and musical traditions."[53]

After participating in two festivals in South Africa, Williams realized that "we were serving all these South African children, but we were not serving any of our young people here." Because community service is "in the spirit of the fraternity," Williams decided to create "the step clinic," which would be an "opportunity to teach the history and development of stepping to young children" and "examine the linkages with dance traditions from around the world, in particular with the gumboot dance." In addition to teaching dance traditions, they "taught them about all kinds of issues around that," such as the "benefits of international travel and college education." The first step clinic was at a school in Savannah, Georgia, in 1996, and since then the fraternity has held them in Georgia, Texas, South Carolina, Ohio, Virginia, and Washington, D.C., as well as in London and Amsterdam. Many young people were stepping, but they "didn't know what they were doing" and "didn't know what these organizations [fraternities and sororities] were"—and they "definitely didn't know about the links between continents." Williams found the step clinics to be a good vehicle for enhancing education.[54]

Since its founding in 1994, Step Afrika! USA has expanded to represent dance traditions other than stepping. Williams wants the group to represent "as many American dance traditions as possible." A performer with the Broadway show *Bring in 'da Noise, Bring in 'da Funk*, Dule Hill, took time off from the show to accompany the U.S. delegation to the South African festival and perform tap. In 1999 Step Afrika! USA brought Maureen Berry from the Maryland-based dance company Footworks to the festival to demonstrate Appalachian clogging and Irish step dancing.[55]

The ability of Step Afrika! to unite dancers on three continents to share dance traditions of Africans and use these traditions for educational purposes illustrates the widespread appeal of stepping. Not only is it performed by religious, community, and school groups but also by dance troupes such as Step Afrika!, the Soweto Dance Theatre, and Tappers with Attitude, another group from Washington, D.C.

Because the founding director of Step Afrika! USA is an alumnus of a black Greek-letter society, he is aware that sharing this Greek performance tradition with non-Greeks is controversial among members. Chapter 5 will examine how Step Afrika! USA selects the elements of stepping that are appropriate to teach to those who are not members of black Greek-letter organizations.

Oral-Formulaic Composition and Stepping

In order to understand how performers adapt to different groups and social settings, it helps to understand the oral composition techniques that facilitate adaptation while retaining tradition. Those familiar with preaching within the traditional black church in America will recognize the use of formulas and themes in oral composition. Many black preachers use formulas and themes to build poetic, powerful messages, which they compose before live audiences and without pen or paper. Bruce A. Rosenberg has found the same techniques of formulas and themes in African American preaching that

Milman Parry and Albert B. Lord found among Yugoslavian epic singers in the 1930s. In *The Singer of Tales,* Lord defined the formula as "a group of words which is regularly employed under the same metrical conditions to express a given essential idea." He also defined the theme as "groups of ideas regularly used in telling a tale in the formulaic style of traditional song." Lord maintained that Homer composed the *Iliad* and the *Odyssey* using formulas and themes. Others, John Foley contends, have applied Lord's theory of oral composition to more than 130 ancient, medieval, and modern traditions. Like the African American traditions of rapping, the blues, and preaching, stepping has strong links to oral-formulaic composition.[56]

Stepping routines are orally composed and transmitted. Adult stepmasters or leaders may teach a routine to younger steppers by "breaking it down" into smaller rhythmic units that the others imitate until they master them. When everyone is the same age, composing a new routine is often collaborative as individuals add new words and movement patterns. Videotapes of step shows circulate widely, aiding in the transmission process. A nationally syndicated stepping competition as well as regional and national meetings of the nine black Greek-letter societies further disseminate steps. Stepping styles vary across the country, and steppers who have lived in several regions can describe stylistic differences. B'Jordan Brookins, who has lived on both the West and East Coasts, observes that at the University of California, Los Angeles, steppers tend to throw punches, with their arms coming over their heads and going straight out. In the South, however, "they come from a waiting motion where both hands are in at the chest and just rolling, and then a straight punch." And in the East, says Brookins, punches "come from around the back with a swing, with a rolling motion and a punch."[57]

Composers draw upon visual and oral formulas and themes. A visual formula and theme may be completely free of a corresponding oral formula or theme or it may be closely tied to it. Visual formulas include repetitions of the hand symbols and bodily icons associated with each fraternity or sorority. For example, forming the index fingers and thumbs of both hands into a pyramid shape refers to Delta Sigma Theta Sorority (fig. 45), whereas raising the arms and holding them above the head, forming a *u*-shape, creates the Greek letter *psi,* the body being the straight line that intersects the *u* (fig. 31). Forming this shape provides an instant, readily recognizable formula for referring to the Omega Psi Phi fraternity. Such visual formulas may complete, punctuate, or comment on a verbal or aural pattern.

A visual theme, on the other hand, is longer in duration and may be named. In 1993 Omega Psi Phi at Southern University in Baton Rouge,

Figure 45. Delta Sigma Theta sisters at Virginia Tech show unity
and their icon, the Pyramid, through their formation and hand
gestures. (Photograph and video by Hazen Robert Walker)

Louisiana, performed the innovative "Midget Step." One person straddles
the other, who is lying on his back, knees bent, and moves his arms and hands
while the supine performer kicks his feet. The illusion is that a very short
person is stepping, and the step embodies the virtuoso essences of stepping—
unity and coordination. Because the step aired nationally on *S.T.O.M.P.*,
steppers throughout the United States quickly imitated the "Midget Step."
The words to the step, as performed by Omega Psi Phi on *S.T.O.M.P.*, come
from a well-known trade step of the Omegas, "Who's That Knocking?":

I say who's that knocking
a knock, knock, knocking,
who's that knocking
at the Que Psi Phi?
Who, who's that knocking at my door?
Why it's the Ques,
trying to break it on down.
I say who's that knocking at my door?
Why it's the Ques,
trying to break it on down.
I say who's that knocking at the door?
Why it's the Ques,
trying to break it on down.
(*The last three lines are repeated three more times.*)[58]

The trade or signature steps performed by chapters throughout the nation convey an organization's ethos and style. Alpha Phi Alpha, priding itself on being the first black Greek organization, imitates old men walking with canes in a counterclockwise circle in "The Grand-daddy." The oral theme, "We're the Alpha brothers, for heaven's sake. / We're the granddaddies making no mistake, / we're the first, the first, and we're never late, / from us all the others originate," accompanies the visual pattern. Alpha Kappa Alpha's trade step, "It's a Serious Matter," expresses pride in their sorority. Arms akimbo, they sweep them both out to the side, as if brushing something off their thighs. At the same time, they step to the right, heads turned sharply to the right, and then to the left, heads turned sharply to the left. While performing these sharp, angular motions, they chant, "Tell me what, what, it's a serious matter." Accompanying verses might relay the history of the sorority or poke fun at other groups. So widely known are both of these steps among black audiences that they alone elicit shouts of recognition.[59]

Examining the new steps composed by Christian and school steppers reveals the oral-formulaic method of composition at work. Using only the visual theme of the "Midget Step," the Anointed Vessels team from the Cornerstone Peaceful Bible Baptist Church in Upper Marlboro, Maryland, ends one routine with two teenaged girls simulating a stepping midget. The teenager moving her arms folds her hands in prayer several times, giving the step a more religious tone. Borrowing only the oral theme of "The Grand-daddy," the Oak Grove African Methodist Episcopal steppers say:

Solo male: He is the
All: King of Kings the greatest of the great,
  He's the almighty making no mistake,
  He's the first, the first, and he's never late,
  from Him all others originate.
  Hit it. (*Virtuoso stepping, with no words.*)
Solo male: Smooth. (*Applause.*)

Using both the oral and visual themes of "It's a Serious Matter," the Troop GOD Steppers from the First Baptist Church of Guilford in Columbia, Maryland, say, "This is a serious matter, / Jesus wants to save your soul. / Accept Jesus Christ, / He will make you whole."[60]

Trade or signature steps, while based on a traditional core, gain power and appeal through variations that reflect an ability to adapt to the audience and theme of a specific occasion. Thus, Alpha Phi Alpha's well-known trade chant "Ice, Ice" (which inspired the white rapper Vanilla Ice's national hit of 1990 "Ice, Ice, Baby") can be used to crack, or to boast, or for more serious purposes. Alpha Phi Alpha, for example, used "Ice, Ice" to boast during a show at the Dance Heritage Festival at East Tennessee State University in Johnson City in 1991:

We are the brothers of A Phi A.
Ice, ice.
We're going to make you a-a-ll say,
"Ice, ice."
And when you see the Black and Gold,
ice, ice,
you know it's gonna be
a heck of a show (*normally* helluva *but censored for the festival*).
Ice, ice.

We're too cold,
we're too darn (damn) cold.
Ice, ice.
We are the brothers of the Black and Gold.
Ice, ice (*twice*).[61]

Adapting "Ice, Ice" to fit the "building bridges" theme of the 1993 *S.T.O.M.P.* competition, Delaware State Alpha Phi Alphas chanted:

Ice, ice.
We are the brothers of black and of gold.
Ice, ice.

We're building bridges for the young and the old.
Ice, ice.
We build them up from the earth to the sky.
Ice, ice.
We build them up with the Lord on our side.[62]

Another popular oral theme is musical, based on the words and tune of an Omega Psi Phi song of love and praise: "All of My Love, My Peace and Happiness, I'm Going to Give It to My Brothers." A high school step team in Blacksburg, coached by an Omega brother, uses the same theme and says, "All of my love, my peace and happiness, I'm gonna to give it to my people." The Eagle Psi Phi step team at Prince Edward High School in Farmville, Virginia, saluted the seniors, juniors, and sophomores and cracked on the freshmen. With each repetition of the "all of my love" theme, they substituted a different class—seniors, juniors, and sophomores. On the fourth repetition, when the audience expected them to say "freshmen," they substituted, "You are not included." In a Christian context, the Mt. Calvary Baptist Church steppers end their entrance step with the same tune and the words: "It's all our love and praise and honor, we want to give it to our savior—Jesus Christ."[63] Well-known spirituals and hymns provide the basis for other musical themes.

A popular oral theme uses a call-and-response rhythmic pattern. The structure is simple but powerful: "When I say X, you say Y. X. 'Y.' X. 'Y.' When I say X, you say Y. X. 'Y.' X. 'Y.' X X. 'Y Y.' X X. 'Y Y.' X X X. 'Y Y Y Y.' X X X. 'Y Y Y Y.'" In Spike Lee's *School Daze,* Dap and Da Fellas move in a counterclockwise circle and use the chant as the basis of a step that disparages the Gammas:

Dap: When I say "Gamma," you say "po."
 Gamma.
All: Po.
Dap: Gamma.
All: Po.
Dap: When I say "Gamma," you say "po."
 Gamma.
All: Po.
Dap: Gamma.
All: Po.
Dap: Gamma Gamma.
All: Po Po.
Dap: Gamma Gamma.

All: Po Po.
Dap: Gamma Gamma Gamma Gamma.
All: Po Po Po Po.
Dap: For the girls in the yard.
All: Yes.
Dap: For the sissies.
All: Q Dogs, yes.
Dap: When I say "Gamma," you say "fag."
  Gamma.
Dap: Fag.
Dap: Gamma.
All: Fag.
(*And so on, repeating structure of the first verse.*)

Repeating this same call-and-response and rhythmic structure, the Oak Grove Steppers, whose leader had seen *School Daze,* chanted:

Leader: When I say "praise," you say "God."
  Praise.
All: God.
Leader: Praise.
All: God.
Leader: When I say "praise," you say "God."
  Praise.
All: God.
Leader: Praise.
All: God.
Leader: Praise praise.
All: God God.
Leader: Praise praise.
All: God God.
Leader: Praise praise praise praise.
All: God God God God.

Tyrone Petty used this same rhythmic theme to keep the audience's attention during a lull in the 1997 "Christian Step Show and FUN-draiser" by leading them in a chant: "When I say Halle, you say 'luia.' Halle. 'luia.' Halle. 'luia.'"[64]

These and similar oral composition techniques enable stepping to spread quickly to new contexts. Drawing on folk, popular, Greek-letter society, and religious traditions, performers can create new routines from familiar patterns.

5 / The Cultural Politics of African American Step Shows

It is a sad fate to see the political and ideological developments of the past fall to tribal dancing and pieces of stone. Oh, do I long for those days of shout'n foot stomp'n tribalism. I long for them to end!
—Kujaliwa Hukumu, *Hilltop*, 5 Nov. 1976, 4

This excerpt from a spirited exchange between Howard University students in 1976 typifies the deep-seated political responses that stepping evokes. Black Greek-letter organizations have from their inception aroused controversy among African Americans. Critics charge the Greek system with fostering elitism and serving the black bourgeoisie and, in the process, causing divisiveness among blacks on college campuses. Proponents praise black Greek-letter societies for encouraging academic and civic ideals, fostering public service, and creating powerful social networks. One might suspect that those supporters would also commend the practice of stepping, but some members of the organizations are critical of it. This chapter examines the cultural politics surrounding stepping. By "cultural politics," I mean the social and political forces that influence what elements of a culture are featured or suppressed, promoted or ignored, sanctioned, or censored.[1]

The Debate over Greek-letter Societies

In order to appreciate differing views about stepping among African Americans, it is necessary first to understand how attitudes vary toward black fraternities and sororities. Because African Americans faced such strong discrimination, many people felt that students should be a united group rather than divided into Greeks and non-Greeks. Class distinctions among African Americans involved the familiar "brown bag and ruler test" and rewarded greater social status to mulattos with whiter skin and straighter hair. Perpetuating these class distinctions among college students seemed foreign to the goals of black colleges.[2]

Further, the religious origins and Victorian values of many black colleges led to strict control over student activities, and only a few literary, debating, and singing groups were allowed to organize. That control persisted through the 1920s in some colleges and into the 1950s in others. Despite the early start at Howard University of five of the nine National Pan-Hellenic Council (NPHC) member organizations, many administrators at other black colleges forbade Greek-letter societies from organizing on their campuses. For example, Paul Quinn College in Waco, Texas, did not permit fraternities on campus until 1951, and Bishop College in Dallas did not allow them until 1954 because "they were concerned that such groups might create a 'class element' on campus, which would be harmful to the growth of the school." Black fraternities and sororities expanded more rapidly at predominantly white institutions, where black students, in the minority, were denied participation in many activities, organizations, and social settings.[3]

Belonging to one of the "Divine Nine" Greek-letter societies signals membership in middle- and upper-class black society. In writing about his experiences among the black upper class, Lawrence Otis Graham says that he has found himself "at a disadvantage" for not joining a black fraternity. "And not surprisingly, to some blacks above the age of fifty, I am 'suspect,' I am seen as being less connected and less committed to the black culture and the 'black struggle.' In conversations at New York business networking events or at Martha's Vineyard summer cookouts, there is inevitably a moment when a host or guest asks the question, 'So, are you an Alpha?'"[4]

The fraternities and sororities that carry the most social prestige are those that were founded earliest, are the largest, and have the wealthiest, most prominent members, Graham observes. Many among "the old-guard black elite would argue that only three of the fraternities—the Alphas, the Kappas, and the Omegas—and two of the sororities—AKAs and the Deltas—actually fit the 'society profile.'" Part of the prestige of belonging to any of the nine organizations stems from the fact that they have exacting requirements for membership, such as "high grade point averages and extensive community service."[5]

Beyond the increased status of fraternity or sorority membership come lifelong associations with like-minded individuals who share a common identity and social values. Graham argues that these organizations "provided a forum, postcollege, through which some of the best-educated blacks in

America can discuss an agenda to fight racism and improve conditions for other less-advantaged blacks."[6]

Not all social critics agree that black Greek-letter societies have been a positive and beneficial social force. *School Daze* (1988), Spike Lee's film portrait of black college life, portrays Greek-letter societies in an unflattering light as sororities vie with each other over skin color and hair styles. Perhaps the most scathing and far-reaching criticism came from the great sociologist E. Franklin Frazier. In *Black Bourgeoisie* (1957), he examined the social, economic, and political life of the black middle class that had developed in the previous two decades. Of the first Greek-letter society for college graduates, Sigma Pi Phi ("the Boulé"), founded in 1904 to bring together "aristocracy of talent," Frazier concluded, "It has become one of the main expressions of social snobbishness on the part of the black bourgeoisie." In assessing on-campus black Greek-letter societies, he noted that they "are especially important in molding the outlook of the black bourgeoisie." Moreover, "membership in these organizations indicates that the student has escaped from his working-class background and achieved middle-class status." Frazier criticized societies for fostering "conspicuous consumption" and their tendency "to divert the students from a serious interest in education." Another problem is that "the leadership and control of these college fraternities are actually in the hands of adult men and women who use the organizations as a source of income." In response to the claims by fraternities and sororities that "they render service to the Negro masses," Frazier argued, the "real spirit of these societies is best represented by the Greek letter fraternity which conducts a campaign for 'Better And Bigger Negro Business.'"[7]

Frazier's analysis echoes Frederick Douglass's 1848 critique of the black fraternal movements of Freemasonry and the Odd Fellows. Although Douglass believed that "some of the best and brightest among us are numbered with those societies," he wanted "to see these noble men expending their time, talents and strength for higher and nobler objects than any that can be attained by weak and glittering follies of odd-fellowship and freemasonry."[8]

More recent studies of the black bourgeoisie have called some of Frazier's findings into question. In 1983 Martin Kilson reevaluated his claims in light of the rapid growth of the black middle class in the 1960s and 1970s and its incorporation into national job markets. Kilson found merit in some of Frazier's insights but argued that his interpretation of the black bourgeoisie "was too one-dimensional, attributing too much significance to social class as such." Frazier "minimized the complex influence of persistent racism upon the self-image of upper-strata blacks." Kilson maintained that "in an era of rising expectations, reinforced by black ethnic militancy, bourgeois blacks paradoxically resent racism even more than they did in the past." Thus, Kilson is "somewhat less pessimistic" than Frazier about "the conservative potential in the black bourgeoisie's self-serving values." He concluded, "In the short run, it seems that its more self-serving and exploitative proclivities vis-a-vis lower-strata blacks are likely to be checked by the bourgeoisie's need to play a leading part in ridding American society of all vestiges of racism."[9]

Daniel C. Thompson reinforced Kilson's findings in a 1986 study of 2,089 graduates of forty-two United Negro College Fund member institutions. The "vast majority" of the graduates in Thompson's study "certainly [did] not fit into the superficial black society of Frazier's formulation." Instead, he said, "They strongly identify with the problems, concerns, and struggles of their fellow black Americans and manifest a compelling feeling of responsibility to set and maintain high moral and ethical standards and to serve as dedicated, effective leaders of institutions, efforts, and programs designed to advance the status and outlook of blacks." Rather than defining the black elite as a snobbish, socially exclusive group, Thompson draws on W. E. B. Du Bois's vision of the "Talented Tenth" of college-educated blacks as well as Thomas Jefferson's concept of a "natural aristocracy" of those "with superior education and talents."[10]

Among the college graduates Thompson studied, 67 percent had joined Greek-letter organizations in college, and 37 percent were active in them after graduation. These organizations "provide effective communication among college-educated blacks," Thompson maintains. Through magazines, newsletters, and regular meetings at the local, regional, and national level, such "effective communication often results in a system of networking whereby 'brothers' and 'sisters' provide mutual aid for each other." Far from being unconcerned with the problems of blacks who are less well-off, Thompson argues that the fraternities and sororities "sponsor well-planned community-related programs, carefully designed to advance the status and quality of life among the black masses. . . . It is ironic," he concludes, that Frazier's *Black Bourgeoisie* was "published on the eve of the powerful civil rights movement which was actually led by middle-class blacks."[11]

Like Thompson, Bart Landry, in *The New Black Middle Class* (1987), also finds some fault with *Black Bourgeoisie*. Landry states that "the criticism that Frazier's study did not rest on systematic and representative empirical data remains true." In addition, Lois Benjamin, in her 1991 survey of one hundred members of the black elite, maintains that "despite the critics, the Talented One Hundred, in general, feel a strong sense of commitment and responsibility for empowering the masses."[12]

Coverage of Greek-letter societies in the Howard University student newspaper and yearbook reveals several different cultural political themes. Evidence from the first few summaries of the Inter-Fraternity Council, established in 1929, suggests that unhealthy competition "inimical to the orderly development of under-graduate life" characterized the early years of fraternal life. The 1932 Inter-Fraternity Council yearbook summary found it "deeply significant" that although Greek-letter societies "in their infancy" were "purely antagonistic and combatant organizations," they had become in a few years "mutually supporting and dependent."[13]

Once the Greek organizations began to cooperate, they developed a political machine that controlled top student offices. Such political dominance caused great resentment among other students. The headline "Greek Political Trust Smashed" filled the entire front page of the *Hilltop* on 17 March 1953. The accompanying story reports that "in a shocking reversal of policy" the student council "threw the Greek Letter organizations out of control of the Grid and May Queen elections and took the now elective offices of the *Hilltop* out of the political arena."[14]

Debates about Greek-letter societies became especially intense in the 1960s and 1970s as the civil rights, black power, women's liberation, and antiwar movements brought more intense political and social awareness to college campuses. Carole Joffe, a student from Brandeis University, spent a week visiting at Howard in 1965 and wrote an article portraying Howard as a conservative institution with "indifferences—in some cases, hostility—to participation in political action." Except for "a small nucleus of politically-oriented students, mainly SNCC workers," who took "leaves of absence to work in Mississippi," Joffe argued, "most of the student body is, by their own admission, party-oriented, and membership in a fraternity or sorority is a mark of prestige in many circles. Even for those who were not Greek there were many parties and dances each weekend. In short, the typical Howard student corresponds quite closely to the middle-class Negro in *Black Bourgeoisie*, by E. Franklin Frazier, head of Howard's sociology department until his death three years ago."[15]

In contrast to Joffe's point of view, Don Royster, chapter editor for Omega Psi Phi fraternity, wrote in 1965 that "Omega and Omega men have been in the forefront of the fight for equality of the Negro." As evidence, he cited an Omega national mandate (issued in 1955) that each graduate chapter take out life memberships in the NAACP. "To date," Royster said, "forty-one of our chapters have life memberships and seventy-three are subscribing." His own Alpha chapter had taken out such a membership in 1964. According to Omega Psi Phi records, between 1955 and 1959 Omega graduate chapters contributed $40,000 to the NAACP.[16]

Although some evidence suggests that membership in black Greek organizations declined in the 1960s, other evidence indicates that the new political urgency of the civil rights struggle invigorated it. "Greekdom is dying!" began Benny J. Pugh, Howard's acting director of student activities, at the opening session of the Greek seminar on 7 March 1965. "My theory is we are not meeting the challenge posed by this era." The seminar was the main feature of the first annual Greek Weekend, organized "to suggest ways and means of strengthening the programs and goals of Greeks."[17]

In contrast to Pugh's death-knell, a report from the executive secretary of Kappa Alpha Psi stated that although white fraternities were undergoing "great losses" during the 1960s, membership in his fraternity had "increased greatly." Twenty-four active chapters were chartered during this period. Indeed, all member organizations of the NPHC played active roles in the civil rights movement. Tom Bradley, Kappa Alpha Psi's grand polemarch, "participated in the discussions which led to the ratification of the Federal Civil Rights Act of 1964, and President Johnson's Anti-Poverty Program." Alpha Phi Alpha brother Martin Luther King, Jr., "was able to garner the large and important resources of the fraternity," which helped "coordinate marches, rallies and fund-raisers for the movement." Other influential Alphas active in the civil rights movement included Andrew Young, Adam Clayton Powell, and Thurgood Marshall. Delta Sigma Theta sorority contributed funds "needed to bail the students out of Southern jails." The social urgency of the civil rights struggle galvanized and inspired twelve students at Morgan State College (now Morgan State University) in Baltimore to start an African American social service fraternity, Iota Phi Theta. Three weeks after the 28 August 1963 March on Washington and King's "I Have a Dream" speech, Iota Phi Theta was organized, and by 1968 it had incorporated as a national fraternity in the state of Maryland. Strongly committed to the African American community, one of its first acts of political action was to boycott a segregated shopping mall in Baltimore. After many years of lobbying, Iota Phi Theta was admitted to the NPHC on 19 November 1996.[18]

Another persistent theme in the controversy over the black Greek system stems from abuses of the pledging system, such as injuries arising from hazing. Before the NPHC replaced pledging with the intake process in 1990 and pledges marched on line and were submissive to big brothers and sisters, critics of pledging often attacked such behavior as demeaning. "I can't see where the Greeks have any relevance to Black people" said a Howard student the *Hilltop* interviewed on the subject of pledging and Greek-letter societies. The student called their tactics "demoralizing" and said, "I myself need not be brutalized or degraded in any manner to become aware of my loyalty and brotherhood to my fellow Black brother." In a front-page *Hilltop* article in 1975 that criticized hazing incidents involving the Alphas, Michael A. Cressey asked, "What is the difference in fighting White America to be free as a race of people and later finding ourselves enslaved by brothers with acts of physical brutality in fraternities?"[19]

"Most of the accusations made were blatant lies," responded E. K. Holman on behalf of the Alphas. "In 1974, Beta chapter's entire program improved so markedly in the succeeding twelve months, including its pledge program, that the group was named the Eastern Region's 'Outstanding College Chapter of the Year.'" Although individual fraternities and sororities tried to eliminate hazing in the 1980s and the NPHC abolished pledging in 1990, the press continues to decry hazing violations around the country.[20]

As Afrocentrism grew in popularity during the 1980s, students at institutions such as Howard and Morehouse College in Atlanta began to question the appropriateness of African American students forming brotherhoods around Greek letters. In "Moving Past Greece to Africa," Chris Madison argues that "because we are entering the twenty-first century and this is 1989 and not 1906, there should be concrete changes issued forth by the younger members. The first would be a name change. We are descendants from the great Shaka Zulu, the fearless warrior Queen Nzingha, and the father of medicine Imhotep, not from Alexander, Plato, and Aristotle." In 1987 students at Morehouse formed "the first definitively Afrikan fraternity," KMT. The letters mean "the black lands" and refer to the original name for Egypt, which translates from hieroglyphics into the English word *Kemet*. Because KMT members "visualize, understand, and study history from an Afrocentric point of view," according to Eddie Glaude, they "thought it would be a contradiction to use Greek letters." Visiting KMT members who spoke about the fraternity at Howard University in 1989 explained, "The Morehouse administration was not very cordial or supportive." Others asked, "What's wrong with a Greek fraternity?" Jeffrey Allen responded, "KMT is not trying to invalidate traditional Greek-letter fraternities" but wanted "to work with our brothers and sisters who are in those organizations."[21]

African-centered fraternities and sororities such as KMT exist throughout the country, and many have step teams and participate in step shows. Malik Sigma Psi, founded in 1977 at C. W. Post College of Long Island University to serve the African Latino community, calls itself "African Fraternalists" and avoids what they label as "Black Greekism." The Web-site of the chapter at Hofstra University features pictures of the Malik Sigma Psi step team.[22]

One answer to Afrocentric criticisms of the use of Greek letters comes from John Berry, a member of Alpha Phi Alpha. "Initially the Greeks were African," posits Berry, so "Greek-lettered fraternities and sororities have a right and reason to represent their respective organizations with Greek letters." Further, Berry argues that the first founders of Alpha Phi Alpha in 1906 used Greek letters as "a mechanism to camouflage their intentions, which included uplifting the African race through service to the community." Because most people who saw black Greek-letter organizations "thought that these organizations had the same intentions as their white counterparts," it "masked from the mainstream of society our true goals and objectives."[23] Despite its use of Greek letters, Alpha Phi Alpha has always cultivated an African identity through use of the Sphinx as its dominant symbol and the use of Egyptian headdresses in many of its public rituals, including stepping.

The Debate over Stepping

As stepping grew in visibility on the Howard campus during the 1970s, a few students strongly criticized the practice. In 1976 Vance Hawthorne, who had just viewed a film about Malcolm X and seen a tribute to Paul Robeson "and a host of others speaking on the crucial issue of Black survival," walked out of Founders Hall, and witnessed the Friday afternoon Greek "demonstrations," the popular word for stepping at the time:

> What is our purpose here? to party, profile, and make a buck? Or to gain the necessary tools for our liberation? If we are not serious, then we should stop kidding ourselves and telling the world we are the Black leaders. What we do on campus now we will be doing out in the "real world.". . . A lot of the energy expended by stomping, chanting and cursing could be used more constructively. On "Demonstration Day" this year, why not demonstrate for the reinstatement of Frances Welsing as a change from parading around like a Barnum and Bailey circus attraction? Black people sure do not need any more family divisions, big or small, and we have far too many entertainers.[24]

The contrast between the serious political issues raised by Malcolm X and the entertaining fun of stepping bothered Hawthorne, and the juxtaposition of stepping with an anti-Apartheid memorial service disturbed Jacqueline Brown. Writing to the *Hilltop* in 1976, she complained that "the brothers of Omega Psi Phi continued their every Friday ritual of demonstrating after repeated attempts to get them to stop."[25]

Echoing those criticisms a few days later, Kujaliwa Hukumu argued, "We don't have time to march around a stone when our people are being systematically 'redlined' out of urban areas." Moreover, he added,

It is contradictory to claim to be Black and greek too. Either you are Black with a Black identity, purpose and direction . . . [or] you are greek. To confuse our identity with another must mean these "greeks" do not recognize our culture as alive, valid, and dynamic as any other in the world. . . .

Lets get back to the work of Liberating our people. If we must march, let us march for African Liberation. If we must shout let us shout for an end to oppression. . . .

It is a sad fate to see the political and ideological developments of the past fall to tribal dancing and pieces of stone. Oh, do I long for those days of shout'n foot stomp'n tribalism. I long for them to end![26]

These and other attacks on stepping and the Greek system prompted a spirited defense by two members of Omega Psi Phi a week later. In a letter to the editor, K. Earl Ferguson and Edward Hailes, Jr., responded to charges that black Greeks do not appreciate black culture and that stepping is not derived from the black experience. They cogently outlined the relevance of stepping to black life:

The Dial, as we call our Friday session of marching is derived solely from the Black Experience; we know nothing of the Greek Experience. The weekly "stomp show" is as real and as relevant as:

—Our ancient tribal tradition of expressing jubilation through song and dance
—Slave songs that are part of our heritage
—Drinking wine and crooning on the neighborhood corner
—The talent and versatility of our people
—The struggle for our right to be heard
—The need to communicate our message
—And the job of expressing our love for one another.
Brutus, forget not from whence you have come.[27]

In the accompanying paid advertisement, Ferguson and Hailes linked leadership skills to the character traits developed through stepping and showed profound understanding of stepping's existential message of strength and unity and of steppers' courage, tenacity, and enthusiasm. Explaining the Omega philosophy of leadership, they argued that theirs was "a leadership that does not assume that it has found a cure for all of life's ills, a leadership that recognizes the deep, intrinsic difficulties involved in social change, that accepts life's often unfavorable odds—but will not stop hoping, or trying, or enjoying when it's possible to enjoy." They explained that stepping (what they called marching and singing) expressed their hopes and developed their leadership abilities:

That hope is what we celebrate each Friday as we march and sing. It is not enough as leaders to merely sketch a vision of our future success. We must prepare our people for the frustration of reaching a high goal, and persuade them that they have the inherent strength within themselves to get there. To accomplish the hard task of bringing black people to their ultimate goal of liberation requires exceptional stamina especially among those who take the lead. We must present externally and internally the courage, tenacity and enthusiasm to overcome the powerful debilitators of self-absolvement, and self-pity.[28]

The Impact of Institutionalization, Expansion, and Commodification

Stepping as an art form underwent significant changes during the last twenty years of the twentieth century. Step shows, which began as esoteric ritual performances seen mostly by other black Greeks, are now popular fund-raising events on college campuses and at community festivals and high schools. Church groups sponsor step teams and competitions, and Latino and Asian Greek-letter societies perform in step shows as well. The public at large has been exposed to stepping through film, television and commercials, and social and political events such as celebrations for the Olympics and President Clinton's inaugural festivities, as well as in such prestigious performance spaces as the Kennedy Center. Promoters develop step shows as money-making events, and corporate advertisers underwrite them in return for advertising opportunities. Entrepreneurs sell videotaped step shows through the Internet. Clearly, stepping has made the transition from folk to popular culture.

While stepping continues to serve its original ritual purposes in black Greek-letter societies, it now serves new functions for new audiences and participants. These rapid developments have led to changes in step show rules and stepping style and debates about stepping's role and the increased commodification of the art.

David Chaney lists four types of pressure that structure cultural politics in the transition from folk to popular culture:

1. commercialization (supplanting amateur production of performance by commercially inspired professionals);
2. suppression (deliberate attempts to stamp out or control what were felt to be illegitimate performances);
3. bourgeoisification (a process in which concern for respectability came to supplant the value of vitality); and
4. alienation (transforming work so that, for the majority, it becomes alienating and has consequential implications for leisure).[29]

When I first wrote about the cultural politics of African American step shows in 1991, I saw only the pressures of suppression and bourgeoisification, or what I call "respectability," as outcomes of the large, institutionalized step shows used as fund-raising events. At the turn of the twenty-first century, it is clear that commercialization is happening as well.

Examining the impact of an institutionalized step show at Virginia Tech reveals in microcosm how similar shows at other campuses may have influenced stepping style and content. In 1983 Virginia Tech students inaugurated a stepping competition to raise scholarship funds in memory of a popular black professor, Overton R. Johnson. The event marked the first institutionalized setting for stepping on campus. Before 1983, stepping was largely spontaneous and all but invisible to the public at large. Black Greek organizations would perform outside dormitories and dining halls or in small auditoriums, but publicity was mostly by word of mouth. With the Overton R. Johnson Endowed Scholarship Step Competition, new forces began to influence the form of stepping:

1. A change of place, from the yard, block, or small auditorium to the largest public auditorium on campus.

2. A change in audience to include members of all the black Greek organizations, black professors, visiting black Greeks from other schools, judges (both black and white), members of the general public, and university administrators.

3. Formalized standards for judging the stepping competition that emphasize appearance, crowd appeal, precision and synchronization, level of difficulty, vocalization, originality, and personality.

In the new setting of the institutionalized step show, free-spirited and sometimes ragged and offensive crack steps seemed magnified in intensity. The first serious problem with cracking occurred in the 1985 Overton R. Johnson Step Competition with a series of hard-hitting cracks by Alpha Kappa Alpha on their chief rival, Delta Sigma Theta sorority.

I was walking cross the yard just as happy as can be,
when a confused little pyramid approached me.
I said, "Are you all right, can I give you a hand?"
She said, "Stop DST." I said, "Don't understand."
I said, "Let me tell you something 'bout my sorority."
She said, "Is it anything like DST?"
I said, "Me, a D a S a T?"

She even had the nerve to call us names.
We're all kind of animals is what they claim.
The sacred pyramid and elephant too.
_____ or to the zoo.

I said, "You steal too much.
Oh Sigma Gamma Alpha,
you know it's hard for you to do that
because you're nothing but a copycat.
But what can we expect from DS thieves?"

The Delta story has now been told,
that your new colors are red and gold.

They even had to go and change their name.

I said, "We're laughing at you.
This is a serious matter."[30]
(*Lines indicate phrases that were unintelligible.*)

As in many cracks, the sisters of AKA play off the DST icon, the Pyramid, and their colors. The lines about colors and name allege that DST at one time had to change their name and colors, which had already been claimed by a white fraternity. But the crack that was most offensive to the Deltas, and which elicited the biggest audience reaction, was, "I said, 'You steal too much. . . . Because you're nothing but a copycat. But what can we expect from DS Thieves?'" An AKA soror maintains that the reference to stealing was because Deltas were believed to copy other sororities' routines. The Deltas, however, took the crack more literally to refer to an embarrassing incident a few days earlier, when Delta sisters had been arrested in a local store for alleged shoplifting.[31]

The hard-hitting cracks had tremendous impact on the Deltas and created long-lasting tensions between the two sororities. In the weeks following the 1985 competition, the president of the Deltas complained at a meeting of black fraternity and sorority presidents that AKA had not showed them respect. In response, AKA picked up the respect issue and turned it into a crack performed in a block show outside a dining hall in the spring of 1986 (fig. 46). The crack was performed to their trade step, "It's a Serious Matter":

Oh Delta Sigma Theta
(Oh DST)
you want respect,
(you want respect,)
but it has to be earned,

(but it has to be earned,)
or you're gonna get burned.
So don't flick my Bic,
a ha ha ha ha ha.
This is a serious matter.
This is a serious matter.[32]

The crack only intensified tensions between the two largest sororities, and many of the relatively small number of black students at the university were aware of the bad feelings between the groups. Consequently, delegates charged with planning the Overton R. Johnson Step Competition drew up rules that prohibited cracking in the 1986 show. Any group that cracked would be eliminated from competition. In the following excerpt from the 1986 show, one can see the adaptive form of trade steps as AKA performed a non-crack and retrospective version of "It's a Serious Matter." The routine recounted the history of the sorority as well as some favorite steps from past shows. The leader stood in the middle of the stage, with a group of sisters standing on each side:

Figure 46. An Alpha Kappa Alpha sister at Virginia Tech chants "It's a Serious Matter" with great intensity. (Photograph and video by Hazen Robert Walker)

Leader: Question.
Stage-right group: Question, we have a question for you.
Stage-left group: Question, we have a question for you.
Leader: I said, what, what? It's a serious matter.
All: What, what? It's a serious matter.
All: What, what? It's a serious matter.
All: In 1908 was our founding date,
All: in '74 we did it once more.
Leader: Tell me.
All: What, what? It's a serious matter.
Leader: Tell me.
All: What, what? It's a serious matter.
(*Group did a nonverbal step and clap routine and repeated the serious matter refrain.*)
All: Nine fine founders at Howard's Miner Hall,
   twelve charter members, and that's not all.
Refrain[33]

When it was the Deltas' turn to perform, they showed every sign of winning the competition until they commenced a none too subtly disguised crack that responded to the respect crack AKA had launched in front of the dining hall:

Oh, Delta Sigma Theta Incorporated
from VPI.
We're here to march, and we're here to step. I said S.O.I.
because you know that we know that you know who you are,
because you're walking round the yard just a-thinking you're a star.
Respect? (*The sorors posed, hands on hips.*)

[Audience member: "Skee wee!"]

And we're laughing at you, and you know why.
You wanted the best, but you settled for less.
I said we're laughing at you, and you know why.
Cause Delta's gonna run it till the day we die.[34]

In response to the crack, an AKA in the audience shouted "skee wee" in a high-pitched voice right after the word *respect*. As an AKA notes, the call signaled judges that the step had been interpreted as a crack.

Each year the Overton R. Johnson Step Competition grows in popularity. The originator of the competition, Calvin Jamison, refers to it as "the Superbowl of block shows" and compares it to a "fine art" and a "Broadway musical." Judges, drawn from faculty and staff, use criteria that do not include skillful cracking. The spontaneity and freaking found outside on the block has largely disappeared, but the rule against cracking in the competition still holds.[35]

Institutionalization has affected the style of stepping in several ways. First, students say, there is greater emphasis on completely nonverbal steps, or what some term "hard stepping." Hard stepping groups strive for intricate, rhythmical moves. On the University of North Carolina campus in Chapel Hill, "hard stepping" does "not necessarily mean hitting the ground hard, but refers to increased emotional intensity." According to Amy Davis, the AKA stepmaster at UNC, because stepping has "gotten so big now" and is in "big auditoriums and they can't really hear your words . . . you really have to do something out there to make them look." By using break dancing and showy acrobatic moves such as leap-frogging or jumping over rolling bodies, steppers aim to captivate the audience (fig. 47). Second, because cracking is forbidden, students have changed traditional crack steps, as when AKA recited sorority history rather than cracks to "It's a Serious Matter." Third, groups use nonverbal and nonderogatory mocking as salutations or tributes. Finally, groups include more skits and singing, which make their performances seem more like variety shows than straight stepping. As one student said, "Once you can't crack, it will have to be more of a show with dancing and singing. Otherwise it will be too boring."[36]

Fortunately for the vitality of stepping at the university, students resist the institutional pressures of suppression and respectability by breaking some rules, as the Deltas did with their cracks in the 1986 show, and by continuing to perform in traditional arenas where such rules are not imposed. The African American verbal dueling tradition is strong, and it is hard to leave a verbal attack unanswered. The AKAs refused to let the Deltas have the last word with their respect crack in the 1986 step competition. At the Black Alumni Weekend the following fall, AKA responded with a new crack sung to the tune of *The Beverly Hillbillies* theme song and performed "It's a Serious Matter":

> The first thing you know there's DST,
> the white man said, "This is my fraternity."
> He said, "I'm going to sue you, and that's the way it be."
> He took them to court, and what do we see—
> red-gold, red-white,
> why the heck can't you get it right?[37]

As stepping moves from the esoteric arena of intergroup shows to public displays for heterogeneous audiences at institutionalized step shows, groups

Figure 47. Dramatic acrobatics are calculated to please the audience, as in this 1990 show by Alpha Phi Alpha at Virginia Tech. (Photograph by Hazen Robert Walker)

tend to suppress cracking. When Kappa Alpha Psi brothers at East Tennessee State University stepped for the Southern Dance Traditions Conference at ETSU in 1990, for example, they chose not to perform crack steps. David Harvin, the fraternity's president, contended that the steps had been omitted because they were inappropriate for a non-Greek audience. A diverse audience would not appreciate the meaning of the cracks, and they might foster the wrong impression. In the public discussion following the step show, after a few rival black Greeks in the audience had hooted at some of the Kappa steps, one Kappa brother said, "I want to make it clear that while we do step and while we talk about other fraternities and they talk about us, . . . that we do get along with the other black Greeks, that there is unity on this campus."[38]

As stepping grew in visibility and popularity, the NPHC developed a policy on step shows in the early 1990s. The policy begins by recognizing the many positive functions of such shows. As "a creative and unique form of artistic and musical entertainment," step shows provide both the university community and the public "a forum to better understand the unique culture (e.g. history and traditions) of Black fraternities and sororities." Because the "language, behavior, and symbols" in step shows "send strong messages," the NPHC argues, "these cultural expressions may also have the potential for individuals to form opinions about the values and beliefs of local fraternities and sororities." Moreover, because "step shows help prospective members become more informed about the organization in which they seek membership," they "have the potential to be a source of marketing Black fraternities and sororities." Another benefit is that step shows "create an environment conducive to intra- and inter-group fellowship," which is especially important to black students "matriculating at predominantly white institutions, where many of these students feel isolated and perceive a lack of emotional support."[39]

The NPHC also recognizes the potential problems that can result from step shows. They should not, the policy warns, "involve the degradation and/ or belittlement of any other Greek-letter organization." In addition, step shows "should not be performed using lewd, indecent, or obscene behavior." Performances of "such reproach" are "not only inconsistent with the inter-fraternal spirit that exists among the NPHC, but also may help perpetuate negative stereotyping of Black fraternities and sororities." Such negative stereotyping "often overshadows the positive philanthropic and other global projects undertaken by the NPHC organizations."[40]

In addition to spelling out inappropriate behaviors, the NPHC policy "strongly" urges undergraduates "to consider positive themes when developing step shows," such as "famous Black contributions to society." If skits are performed in a show, "they should be developed to convey positive political, social justice, and moral messages." In an effort to facilitate such positive themes, the "NPHC invites local councils and affiliated organizations to send creative, alternative step show ideas to its National Headquarters for widespread exchange of artistic and musical expression."[41]

While suppressing cracking may blunt the potential for stepping to create or redress a breach or crisis in the social drama of black Greek life (chapter 2), stepping, even without cracking, remains a lively, fundamentally competitive performance tradition. As one Kappa brother from East Tennessee State University said at the Southern Dance Tradition Conference in 1990, "We mainly step to show the other fraternities that we are the best."[42]

Many members of black Greek-letter organizations are keenly aware of the issues raised by the increasing popularity of stepping. Some, such as Darryl R. Matthews, Sr., former executive director of Alpha Phi Alpha, fear that stepping "has become a substitute for the lack of academic leadership among our people on the college campus. . . . When chapters can't figure out anything credible to do, they step." Matthews provoked a lively debate on the NPHC list-serv by speculating on what would happen if other competitions replaced step shows:

> What if we had competition between BGLO's (Black Greek Lettered Organizations) that showcased our academic prowess? What if we had a "brain bowl" competition between the BGLO's? What if we had oratorical contests where the themes were based on providing practical solutions to problems confronting our communities? What if we had teams made up, from our respective BGLO chapters, that quantified and spent the same number of hours we now spend in step practice to compete in a business plan writing competition? Why we might even find some of the ventures from the competitions worthy of funding. Better yet, we might even begin to experience community self determination, creating jobs and becoming producers instead of conspicuous consumers. Are these whack ideas, or will we just keep on shuffling, stomping, and buck dancing, thereby reducing the prestige of our venerable organizations to mere entertainment?[43]

Matthews is not alone in his concern about the growing popularity of stepping eclipsing the public-service functions of the organizations. Amy Davis reports that "as white America grows more aware of stepping through mass media and campus activities, the fraternal organizations worry that this notoriety may overshadow other community services they perform."[44]

Frank Mercado-Valdes, producer of the syndicated television program *S.T.O.M.P.*, says that although he enjoys the support of some national offices of Greek-letter societies, others do not approve of the show. "We have received criticism because the idea has been that stepping has been just one element of Greekdom and . . . some fraternities and sororities have not wanted to have that element so visible in the forefront." Mercado-Valdes believes these critics do not understand that his program, through dialogues with the emcees and vignettes, is a vehicle for educating viewers about black Greek life. Fraternities and sororities can use stepping as colleges use winning sports teams—to attract students. Because he is a Greek himself, Mercado-Valdes would like to restrict the show to the original black fraternities and sororities, although he would consider other stepping groups. "But we are not sure where *S.T.O.M.P* the television show will go," he says. "At the moment it looks like the Greek angle is the angle, but we certainly are open, especially if the process opens up, or particularly if the Greek organizations continue to stonewall us. We may have no choice but to open it up and bring stepping as more of a mass vehicle and let them know they're not the only ones; they don't own stepping."[45]

The question of the "ownership" and commodification of stepping leads to issues of cultural politics as participants contend over who constitutes legitimate performers and what constitutes the proper audiences, styles, and social uses of the art form. Two graduate students from Howard University, B'Jordan Brookins, a member of a graduate chapter of Omega Psi Phi, and Allison Cotton, in a graduate chapter of Delta Sigma Theta, provide insight on the increasing commodification of stepping and its expansion into non-Greek and non-African American venues. When Cotton described Alpha Phi Alpha brothers who had made soft-drink and shoe commercials, Brookins replied, "People are making millions of dollars off of us and it's not coming into the organizations." At issue is that, as Cotton says, "the purpose [of stepping] is only part entertainment." Stepping is about "camaraderie and tradition," and it is "sacred" to their organizations. Although Cotton recognizes that black Greek organizations have commodified stepping by organizing large competitions and charging admission, she maintains, "It's different when it's in the African American community because we don't have the money and the power to exploit it to the extent that television can. When we take money from ticketholders, it's going into our scholarship programs, for example, so we're putting money back into the community." "That's where the anger is coming in," Brookins adds. "I think that these people are making millions of dollars off of stepping, and it's not coming back into the community. . . . because you've got to remember . . . that the tenets of our organizations are our community service."[46]

In discussing the popular percussive performance group called *Stomp!* that has appeared on numerous television shows and commercials, both students noted that the group has borrowed material from black Greek steppers:

> C: When I saw the *Stomp!* group, I could pick out aspects of Omega, I could pick out aspects of Alpha because there are different personalities that go into their stepping.
>
> B: It's really nice, but it's borrowed. And these people are going to get all the national recognition from this and people aren't even going to know its roots. Everybody's going to say, "Oh yeah, they're doing what they did," and really in essence they're doing what we've always been doing, or we've already done.[47]

Aware that whites are beginning to pick up stepping, Cotton adds, "To be perfectly honest, I do not want the white community to get a hold of it. It's a traditionally African, black thing, and I will hate the day when I see Kappa Alpha Theta or Pi Kappa Phi or one of the other sororities from a white university stepping. I'll have a huge problem with that. Huge."

Expressing a similar attitude, in 1992 a member of Alpha Phi Alpha at Longwood College in Farmville, Virginia, objected to a white sorority's request to teach them to step. Although some of his brothers felt it was all right to teach the generic steps, he said, "The only two things black people have left are the black church and stepping." African Americans "should not give away [their] secrets or throw away something precious." His hesitation may have been affected by the controversy among blacks about a then-popular white rapper, Vanilla Ice, whose hit "Ice, Ice, Baby" was based on the refrain of one of Alpha Phi Alpha's well-known chants.[48]

In the process of teaching stepping to children, members of Step Afrika! USA have had to examine what parts of the their Greek stepping tradition are appropriate to share with non-Greeks. As Brian Williams, founding director of Step Afrika! USA, notes, "Greeks were not cool about sharing the tradition of stepping. It was something that we kind of kept to ourselves. And we were offended when someone was trying to do a similar movement. And we had to go through a lot because we were teaching this dance in Africa but we weren't as willing to teach it in the States."[49]

Once they started to view stepping as "our culture we were sharing," they decided to "share a certain part of the tradition," including its "history and development." Williams makes clear what parts of stepping are sacred and not taught to outsiders:

> Some of what we do is considered sacred, like the difference between show steps and yard steps. We'll teach a show step, but you would never see us teaching . . . steps that you do on campus in a circle, the circle steps. . . . And of course, we never teach children to say Alpha Phi Alpha or shout out our fraternity name. We always adjust the step to their conditions. So if we are stepping . . . in MLK high school, or an elementary school, instead of saying A Phi A, we'll say MLK. And in Africa when we teach, we'll say Af-ri-ca as opposed to A Phi A. I think its our attempt to respect the tradition and its origins and how Greeks feel about it, . . . but then still allow us to share it as a cultural tradition.[50]

Other sacred parts of the Alpha stepping tradition that Williams would not teach to others include the fraternity's national hymn and its call. He believes it is appropriate to teach a signature step such as "Ice, Ice, Baby," but with altered words, as long as that signature step is not a circle step.

While Step Afrika! teaches stepping to children and adults who are not black Greeks, teaching stepping is a means to greater ends, such as establishing a dialogue. "Stepping was a way for me to get a dialogue started with these brothers from Lesotho and share something," Williams says, "like sharing some food. . . . And then from that, we can do all kinds of stuff. The purpose is not just to dance, the purpose is the larger project of cross-cultural exchange and long-term dialogue."[51]

Just as the Soweto Dance Theatre, which hosts the Step Afrika! International Festival, "performs dance works that have themes with an educational content such as environmental awareness and social political issues," many step teams formed by churches and community groups use stepping to instill social values such as respect, obedience, discipline, and hard work. At the end of their stepping workshop at the Kennedy Center, choreographer Kirsten Smith led the children in a call-and-response pledge that stressed the values necessary to become an honorary member of Step Afrika! and "earn the right to step":

> (*Smith and children.*)
> As an honorary member
> of Step Afrika!
> I pledge to respect all adults
> as well as my schoolmates
> and my family and friends,
> to conduct myself
> as the special person
> that I *know* I am,
> and to learn all I can
> about African and American history.

> (*Smith, speaking to children.*)
> Congratulations, you are now honorary members of Step Afrika! and have earned the right to step.[52]

Like other popular African American cultural expressions such as slang, rap, and the blues, stepping may become widely commercialized and adopted by non-African Americans. "If it becomes too commercialized," says Brookins, African Americans will move away from it . . . or we will change it to such an extent that it's not recognizable in its original art form. You'll be able to see the roots in it, but it will transcend. Just like with our slang, when other cultures pick it up, we drop it."[53]

Mirroring the concerns of Brookins and Cotton, Ilyasah N. Upshaw, the first stepping coach of the Oak Grove Steppers, although not a Greek herself, worries that the spread of stepping to non-Greek performers may weaken the respect it deserves: "I'm teaching it [stepping], and I'm not even a Greek. I sometimes am embarrassed about that. How dare me [laughs] come out here and represent something that I don't even belong to. It seems to me that the respect for it is gone. The respect for secrecy, of having something of their very own."[54]

Conclusion

Members of black Greek-letter organizations as well as non-members are concerned about how best to use the power their societies have. Spike Lee, E. Franklin Frazier, and other critics have denounced behaviors that lead to self-aggrandizement, divisiveness, and movement away from social uplift. Scholars such as Martin Kilson, Daniel C. Thompson, Bart Landry, and Lois Benjamin, who have investigated the values and actions of the black bourgeoisie, have disputed Frazier's critique, finding strong evidence of social commitment and action. In assessing some of the criticisms of black Greek-letter organizations Lawrence Ross concludes, "In some ways, those arguments are absolutely right. As with any organization, things don't always work smoothly, nor do the ideals of the organization always trickle down to each individual member. The fraternities and sororities don't promise that they will have a perfect organization. What the fraternities and sororities do promise is that the greater body will make an effort to strive toward their lofty ideals. And this alone makes the Divine Nine organizations relevant and indispensable."[55]

Some of the strongest warnings against a too-strong emphasis on the entertainment dimension of stepping come from within black Greek-letter organizations themselves. Criticism of the amount of time groups spend stepping may reflect the influence of Puritan values that hold dance and entertainment at odds with serious commitment to social change. Yet many leaders of newly developed step teams for schools, churches, and community groups are alumni of black fraternities and sororities, and they use stepping as a way to foster moral education, leadership, character, and community development.

"Stepping is the *now* thing," says teenager Nikki Tennyson of Roxbury, Massachusetts. The 1990s were an explosive period in the evolution of stepping. The change from an esoteric, in-group ritual to a mass-mediated popular art form became a two-edged sword. On the one hand, it brought new attention and praise to the nine African American Greek-letter societies. Stepping has become an important and attractive recruitment vehicle for the societies. On the other hand, as stepping is commodified by others, some members of Greek-letter societies feel it has been cheapened and that the purposes of their organizations have been misrepresented. They are afraid that their organizations, which they know to be about much more than entertainment, will be reduced in the popular mind to only that and not be recognized for social uplift and service. In an attempt to avoid exploitation, some national offices prohibit chapters from participating in commercial step shows without permission from headquarters. Frank Mercado-Valdes, however, believes that "they [the nationals] don't own stepping." Whether anyone can own or control a performance tradition that by its very nature involves innovative compositions remains an issue for further discussion.[56]

Certainly, the pressures of competing before a larger, more heterogeneous, audience have wrought changes in types of routines. Many stepping competitions rule out cracking for fear that audience response might become too heated or that the public will misunderstand the intent of the performers. In an effort to counter the common perception that fraternities and sororities fight among themselves, many shows espouse the goal of unity among all black Greeks. Thus, cracking in such public contexts is frowned upon. Unable to rely on the crowd-pleasing tactics of verbal dueling, since the 1980s many performers have emphasized intricate precision stepping to complex rhythms, or what some students term *hard stepping.*

Pressures to perform well and win (often for large cash prizes) have resulted in increased spectacle and elaborate costumes, gymnastics, and stunts. The traditional circular patterns of the 1950s are rarely seen except in signature steps such as the Alphas' "The Grand-daddy." The circle was conducive to a ritual performance signifying bonding, unity, and communication, and when done publicly, circle steps were often performed around a sacred object such as a monument, sundial, or tree. When transplanted to a stage in an auditorium, and with judges and spectators to please, it seems only natural that the focus of stepping would shift, as it did, to rows of performers facing the audience. Perhaps, too, like Brian Williams from Step Afrika!, other brothers and sisters distinguish between show and yard steps and associate circle steps with sacred rituals that would be inappropriate for large audiences.

Epilogue:
Soulstepping

B: You know, this is like the birth of the blues or the
birth of jazz, and it's going to become a world-wide
phenomenon.

C: But I don't like that. I just want to go on record to say,
I don't like that it's gaining popular support because it
diminishes the importance of the traditional aspect. It's
not meant to appeal to the general public as a fad.
Some aspects of Greekdom are sacred, and stepping is
one of those aspects.

—B'Jordan Brookins and Allison Cotton, Howard
University, 1995

"We're the soulstepping sorors of AKA" sing steppers in a show at Virginia Tech. "We're soulstepping divas" chant a Latino step team of Omega Phi Beta sisters. More than any other word, *soulstepping* encapsulates the power of stepping to express the lived experience, cultural history, and hopes of African Americans and others who identify with their culture. Within the traditional movements and sounds of an African American step show, both performers and spectators participate in celebrating cultural heritage and identity. Clapping hands and stomping feet echo the rhythms of patting juba and ring shouts, dances in which slaves, forbidden to use drums, created elaborate rhythmic patterns with hands, feet, and voices. Military-style commands, postures, facial expressions, and marches evoke the black drill teams that were fostered by African-inspired mutual aid societies that began as early as the eighteenth century and flourished at the time the first black Greek-letter societies were formed in the early twentieth century. They also suggest the disciplined organization, unity, and grit that it has taken for African Americans to withstand the hardships of prejudice and racism. Many songs in step shows evoke spirituals, whose tunes and lyrics form the basis of many fraternal and sororal songs. Those attuned to African dance traditions and art recognize a deeper cultural legacy in stepping—an African aesthetic that manifests itself in all the ways Robert Farris Thompson identified in dance and sculpture in West and Central Africa. Not only do audiences recognize cultural movement patterns but they may also feel a common spirit that unites them with the steppers.

When Brian Williams of Step Afrika! USA first saw a young person doing a gumboot dance in Africa, both the movements and the spirit that animated the dancer seemed familiar. The word *soulstepping* suggests a positive identification with all the nuances implied when African Americans speak of soul music, soul food, and a culture of soul.

Not only does stepping link African Americans to their early history in America and their older roots in Africa, but it also carries a record of the popular movement and musical traditions of the twentieth century. One of the early terms for stepping among Omega Psi Phi fraternity was "hopping," and photographs show Omegas at Howard University in 1969 doing the "Omega Bop" and kicking in a manner reminiscent of the lindy hop. Capturing Motown movements and tunes, steppers might imitate the movements and songs of the Temptations. From hip-hop culture, steppers borrow rapping and breakdancing. In addition, they draw on childhood handclap games and street rhymes. As stepping has grown in popularity, it has influenced popular culture, notably through the hit tune "Ice, Ice, Baby," which was modeled on a signature step of Alpha Phi Alpha fraternity.

Step shows are engaging because they link participants with elements of their cultural heritage and break new cultural ground as steppers innovate. Strobe lights, fog machines, special sound effects, the latest popular music, and virtuoso moves such as stepping while blindfolded all reveal a competitive drive to captivate audience attention. Thus, audiences expect to see not only traditional steps but also something new.

Unlike most other dance forms, African American step shows often demonstrate the power of speech to further inspire participants. In retrospect steps, performers evoke ancestors as they recite the history of their group's formation and name its founders. "Cooper, Coleman, Love, and Just / they are watching over us," sang the brothers of Omega Psi Phi in a show at Virginia Tech. "In 1908 was our founding date, in '74 we did it once more" chanted the sisters of Alpha Kappa Alpha in another Tech show. Indeed, it *is* "a serious matter" to keep alive and celebrate the formation of powerful African American organizations that work on a wide variety of social issues such as civil rights, health care, housing, and mentoring young people.

Church stepping teams recite Bible verses and testify their faith, conveying spiritual commitment through the energy of their stepping. Working for social change, steppers may chant about the need for unity, or the importance of stopping violence, or other social issues. Thus, stepping has great potential as a persuasive device. Recognizing that power, advertisers have turned to step teams to promote their products, and youth workers have employed stepping to promote positive social values in those they mentor.

In trying to pinpoint the great appeal of stepping, I find Stephen Henderson's concept of "mascon imagery" useful. Deriving "mascon" from a NASA acronym that refers to a massive concentration of matter beneath the surface of the moon, Henderson applies the term to the imagery in black poetry and speaks of a "massive concentration of Black experiential energy."[1] Concentrating references to both past and present cultural events, and with allusions to songs, dances, games, and styles, stepping powerfully enacts the sounds and movements through which African Americans have expressed themselves. Through mascon imagery, stepping is both poetry and motion and poetry in motion, a performance art well-suited for many ritual purposes.

Step shows originated in the rites of passage of brotherhoods and sisterhoods of young black college students. But they have been adapted to other ritual occasions as well, whether weddings, funerals, festivals such as the annual Philadelphia Greek Picnic, or church services. Perhaps one reason step shows have grown in importance is that they both enact and stimulate stages of the ritual process, such as liminality and communitas. Fraternal and sororal steppers often enact stages of the pledging process, especially in the probate or neophyte shows in which new members make debuts. Marching in line during a show recalls the earlier pledging ritual of marching on line to demonstrate the new unity of brotherhood or sisterhood. The amount of work necessary to perform complex rhythmic patterns in unison may entrain the biological rhythms of steppers so at the deepest level—the level of the heart—they are truly moving as one. The solemn, stoic expressions of grit on their faces evokes the earnest seriousness of new pledges in a liminal stage. Moreover, the joyful cheers and warm embraces among the audience as they respond to the steppers and greet each other attests to the strong communitas that stepping can build.

Perhaps one reason stepping has grown so popular, both on and off campus, is that it fills a deep need for ritual. Once the intake process replaced the pledging process in 1990, stepping became one of the only public rituals that fraternity and sorority members could perform. Even before pledging was eliminated among NPHC members in 1990, ritual elements of the process, such as going on line, were no longer permitted on many college campuses. Stepping may have increased in popularity among students in black Greek-letter organizations as other venues for public ritual expression disappeared.

Some black Greeks who stepped in the 1950s and 1960s do not believe that stepping originated in Africa, but many younger members do. It is possible that as Afrocentrism gained popularity in the 1980s and 1990s steppers began to identify their moves with African roots, and they added African movement patterns such as the South African gumboot dance and Zulu dances. Although Africans and African Americans have exchanged music and dance traditions for more than a hundred years through such intercultural exchanges as the Virginia Jubilee Singers in the 1890s and Reuben T. Caluza's African Quartette in the 1930s, the process intensified during the late twentieth century as more and more African Americans traveled to Africa and dance troupes throughout the United States performed African dances such as gumboot.

Like other art forms, stepping has been criticized by those who see it as a preoccupation with entertainment and style at the expense of dedicating energy to social leadership and change. Some worry that the attention stepping brings to African American organizations perpetuates stereotyped images of blacks as entertainers. But in a spirited defense of their weekly ritual of stepping, which they call "marching and singing," Howard University students K. Earl Ferguson and Edward Hailes, Jr., in 1976 argued that stepping expresses hope and develops the character necessary for leadership. The difficulty, challenge, and stamina necessary for stepping mirror the "intrinsic difficulties involved in social change." Ferguson and Hailes's defense of stepping suggests that it is a social drama that enacts leadership qualities of "courage, tenacity, and enthusiasm" that must be presented "externally and internally" in order "to overcome the powerful debilitators of self-absolvement, and self-pity." Many schools, churches, community groups, mentoring projects, and organizations such as Step Afrika! use stepping as a way of instilling discipline, strength, team spirit, and community involvement. Such groups view stepping as a means for social change rather than a means for entertainment.[2]

The phenomenal growth of African American stepping and its spread to new venues and performers parallels other African American art forms such as the blues. This rapid growth has caused some members of African American fraternities and sororities to consider the meaning of stepping. There is tension between the pull of a sacred tradition closely identified with fraternal, sororal, and African American identity and its popularization and spread to other contexts.

During the conservative social and political period of the last quarter of the twentieth century, many African Americans experienced heightened racism. On predominantly white campuses, Asra Q. Nomani notes, black undergraduates "are increasingly inclined to bond together, students say, in part because of rising racial tensions on campuses." He says that one black student at Northwestern University (who left the white fraternity he pledged his freshman year to join Alpha Phi Alpha) views stepping more symbolically: "'We show that the only way we're going to make it through here is if we stick together.'" Nomani adds that "blacks seek solace from the black community, and social events such as step shows are at the heart of that." He quotes the same Alpha Phi Alpha student, who says, "'When you walk into a gymnasium and see hundreds of black students, you realize that you do have a support group.'" For those who feel "bombarded with stuff from white America," stepping provides an artistic way to express their history. Other minority groups that have adopted stepping, such as Latino and Asian American fraternities and sororities, find it equally powerful in asserting their unity and identity.[3]

As the cultural identity movements of the 1960s and 1970s expanded to incorporate more communities, and as globalization, the Internet, and satellite communication expose Americans to a wide array of cultures, perhaps the need to demonstrate identity via bold, feisty, foot-stomping stepping is particularly satisfying. As minorities in a country that has a long history of racism, African Americans, Latino Americans, and Asian Americans perhaps sometimes feel that they must walk softly to avoid trouble. At a step show, however, they can proudly celebrate their culture and heritage in the most emphatic way possible, with clapping hands and stomping feet.

Appendix:
Persons Interviewed

All interviews are tape-recorded unless otherwise noted.

Aldaño, Anthony. Telephone interviews with author, 25 May, 31 July, 4 Aug. 1999.

Allen, Sadie. Telephone interview with author, 21 June 1999.

Alpha Kappa Alpha Sorority. Personal interview with author, 9 Feb. 1990, notes. University of South Florida, Tampa.

———, Member 1. Personal interview with author, 18 Oct. 1986. Blacksburg, Va.

———, Member 2. Telephone interview with author, notes, 1986.

Bahbahani, Nada. Telephone interview with author, 25 Aug. 1999.

Brookins, B'Jordan. Personal interview with author, 26 May 1995, Howard University, and telephone interview with author, 18 June 1996.

———, and Allison Cotton. Personal interview with author, 26 May 1995. Howard University.

Cummings, Robert J. Personal interview with author, 2 June 1995. Howard University.

Davis, Anne Mitchem, Personal interview with author, 25 May 1995. Howard University.

Dixon, Dwayne. Telephone interview with author, 3 Dec. 1998.

Fitzgerald, Lora. Telephone interview with author, 13 July 2000.

Ford, Johnny. Personal interview with author, 2 June 1995. Howard University.

Gordon, Michael V. W. Telephone interview with author, 10 Mar. 2000.

Green, Bishop Samuel L. Telephone interview with author, 22 July 1999.

Gumbs, Tameka. Telephone interview with author, 6 July 1996.

Harville, Thomas. Personal interview with author, notes, 4 Mar. 1990. Johnson City, Tenn.

Harvin, David. Personal interview with author, notes, 3 Mar. 1990. East Tennessee State University, Johnson City.

Henderson, Stephon D. Personal interview with author, 25 May 1995, Howard University, and e-mail correspondence with author, 18 Sept. 2000.

Herndon, Michael K. Personal interviews with author, 14 July 1999. Blacksburg, Va., and, notes, 4 Feb. 2000.

Hudgens, Quentin L. Telephone interview with author, 20 Apr. 1997.

Ingram, Rev. Jessica. Telephone interview with author, 17 June 1996.

Jamison, Calvin. Personal interview with author, Mar. 1986. Virginia Tech.

Johnson, Jeff. E-mail correspondence with author, 17 Mar. 2000.

Kulkarni, Nihar Harihar. Telephone interview with author, 30 Mar. 2001.

Matthews, Darryl R., Sr. E-mail correspondence with author, 13 Apr. 1998.

Mercado-Valdes, Frank. Telephone interview with author, 10 June 1996.

Middleton, Pam. Telephone interview with author, notes, 6 Oct. 1995.

Mokhtar, Tamer. Personal interview with author, 17 May 1996. Blacksburg, Va., and telephone interview with author, notes, 27 May 1997.

Muhammad, Galen. Telephone interview with author, 12 July 2000.

Nance, C. Kemal. Telephone interview with author, notes, 20 May 1996.

Nguyen, Trang. Telephone interview with author, 10 Nov. 1999.

Petty, Tyrone C. Telephone interview with author, 19 July 1999.

———, and David H. Smith. Personal interview with author, 16 May 1997. Washington, D.C.

Phi Beta Sigma Fraternity, Mu Nu Chapter, Virginia Tech. Personal interview with author, 1 Feb. 1998. Samuel Henry, Timothy Young, Miley Craig Peppers III, and Saeed T. Richardson.

Ross, Lawrence. Telephone interview with author, 21 July 1999.

Semela, Mbuyiselwa. J. (Jackie). Personal interview with author, 22 Jan. 2000. Washington, D.C.

Sensabaugh, Carter. Personal interview with author, notes, 1988. Blacksburg, Va.

Sigma Gamma Rho Sorority, Kappa Psi Chapter, Virginia Tech. Personal interview with author, 15 Feb. 1998. Deanna McCall, Donna Woodson.

Sumner, Marsha. Telephone interview with author, 22 Jan. 1998.

Terry, Aaron C. Telephone interview with author, 29 Oct. 1999.

Upshaw, Ilyasah Nikkia. Telephone interview with author, 19 June 1996.

Vargas, Jeffrey. Telephone interview with author, 16 Aug. 1999.

Wiley, Geraldine A. Telephone interview with author, 21 July 1999.

Wiley, Jacinta Novine. Telephone interview with author, 14 Aug. 1999.

Wiley, Javitta Lavine. Telephone interview with author, 21 July 1999.

Williams, Brian. Telephone interview with author, 14 Jan. 2000.

Woodruff, Paul. Telephone interview with author, 5 Jan. 2000.

Zeta Phi Beta Sorority, Upsilon Lambda Chapter, Virginia Tech, 1 Oct. 1997. Angela L. Tarry, LaTonya Hucks.

Notes

Introduction

1. Freeman and Witcher, "Stepping into Black Power," 46. The nine historically black fraternities and sororities composing the National Pan-Hellenic Council take pride in their incorporated status. For reasons of economy of space, however, I have chosen to omit the designations *Inc.* or *Incorporated* when referring to a sorority or fraternity in the text.

2. Public comments by Victoria Yuzvenko at the international conference "Oral Epic: Ethnic Traditions and Performance," 10 Sept. 1997, Kiev, Ukraine; Malone, *Steppin' on the Blues,* 188.

3. Nelson, "Stepping Lively," C1, C8.

4. Ross, *Divine Nine,* 425.

5. Ibid.

6. Fine, "Stepping, Saluting, Cracking, and Freaking," 39–59. In using the term *stepping acts* I am referring to things one does with stepping, mirroring speech act theory, developed in Austin, *How to Do Things with Words;* Malone, *Steppin' on the Blues;* Davis, "'Deep in My Heart,'" 83–95; Rouverol, "'Hot,' 'Cool,' and 'Getting Down,'" 96–108; Yarger, "'That's . . . Where Stepping Came From,'" 109–19; Freeman and Witcher, "Stepping into Black Power"; and Nomani, "Steeped in Tradition," A1, A4.

7. Foster, *Reading Dancing;* Ness, *Body, Movement and Culture,* 236; Novack, *Sharing the Dance;* Ness, *Body, Movement and Culture,* quotation on 239 (emphasis in the original), 15.

8. Albright, *Choreographing Difference,* 154.

9. Clifford, *Predicament of Culture.* My reading of stepping as a cultural predicament is influenced by Ness, *Body, Movement, and Culture.*

10. A 1995 National Endowment Summer Stipend provided support for intensive research in the Moorland-Spingarn Research Library and for oral-history interviews at Howard University.

11. Concerned with student safety and fearing litigation over hazing practices, in 1990 the National Pan-Hellenic Council, a confederation of the historically Afri-

can American fraternities and sororities, decided to replace the pledging process with a "membership intake process." Pledging was eliminated as a requirement for initiation, and "lines" and hazing were prohibited. Turner, *Ritual Process,* 95–96.

12. On many college campuses, sweetheart or support organizations composed of members of the opposite sex formed around the various chapters of the nine members of the NPHC. Although neither the NPHC nor the national organizations of the nine constituent organizations condone or support these auxiliary organizations and have taken steps to sanction chapters that encourage them, many sweetheart organizations still exist. For example, a Web-site of the Alpha Angels stated, "It has been said that Angels/Sweethearts are 'illegal' or they do not exist, yet their presence is certainly felt on college campuses across the country." <http://www.members.tripod.com/blackandgold/~index1.html> accessed on 20 April 2001. The site lists forty-five colleges and universities that have Alpha Angels organizations.

13. Frazier, *Black Bourgeoisie.*

Chapter 1: A History of Stepping

1. Petty and Petty and Smith interviews; Fine, "Stepping, Saluting, Cracking, and Freaking," 40.

2. Clifford, *Predicament of Culture,* 1–17; Ross, *Divine Nine,* 6.

3. Wesley, *History of Alpha Phi Alpha,* xiii; Malone, *Steppin' on the Blues,* 168; Wesley, quoting Callis, in *History of Alpha Phi Alpha,* xiii.

4. Wesley, *History of Alpha Phi Alpha,* 21; Malone, *Steppin' on the Blues,* 177; Ross interview. For more on movement traditions in white and black Masonic societies, see Rich, "Freemasonry, the Greeks, and Stepping."

5. Malone, *Steppin' on the Blues,* 186, 167.

6. Ishmail Conway, "It's More Than Stepping," public lecture, Virginia Tech, 28 Feb. 2000. See also Conway, "It's More Than Stepping"; and Wesley, *History of Alpha Phi Alpha,* 75.

7. Malone, *Steppin' on the Blues,* 198–202. For a history of each of the nine fraternities and sororities composing the National Pan-Hellenic Council, see Ross, *Divine Nine.*

8. Ross, *Divine Nine,* 423–24.

9. Iota Phi Theta, Inc., Web-site <http://www.iotaphitheta.org> accessed on 20 April 2002.

10. "Negro Group Initiates Two White Women."

11. Ross, *Divine Nine,* 425.

12. Ibid., 217.

13. Zeta Phi Beta interview. The dog is not an official symbol of Omega Psi Phi, and the national office discourages canine imagery in association with the fraternity.

14. Clifford, *Predicament of Culture,* 15–16.

15. Taylor, "Hell-Week," 3. The Moorland-Spingarn Research Center is missing the *Bison* for 1926 and those for 1934–42.

16. Smith, "Why Walk in a Line?" 30.

17. "Inter-fraternalism at Howard University"; "The Inter-Fraternity Council," 113.

18. *Bison* (1947), 105.

19. "Campus Candids," *Bison* (1950), 74–75; "Greeks before the Camera," *Bison* (1955), n.p.; *Bison* (1957), 80; "Greek Activities," *Bison* (1958), 94–95.

20. *Bison* (1964), 271, 275.

21. *Bison* (1965), 203; Black, "'Why Do We Exist?'" 6. Although the fraternity is unnamed in the caption for figure 8, a similar photograph on the Alpha Phi Alpha page (210) allows the group to be identified as Alphas.

22. *Bison* (1966), 177.

23. Giles, "Greeks Ignore," 2; *Bison* (1969), 221.

24. *Bison* (1970), 184, 187; Johnson, "It's Greek Time Again," 6. Three relatively new social organizations appeared in the Greek section of the 1974 *Bison* (67, 73): Groove Phi Groove Social Fellowship, Swing Phi Swing Sorority, and Wine Psi Phi Fraternity. These non-exclusive groups arose out of the social activism of the 1960s and 1970s and criticism of the exclusivity of traditional black Greek-letter societies. Pictures in subsequent *Bisons* indicate that Groove Phi Groove participates in step shows.

25. *Bison* (1976), 23; Hukumu, "Black 'Greeks' Confuse," 4.

26. Malone, *Steppin' on the Blues*, 205.

27. *Bison* (1977), 120–21; Thompson, *African Art in Motion*, 13–14; *Bison* (1977), 122–23; *Bison* (1978), 242–44; no commentary accompanies the 1977–78 pictures.

28. "Partying Like It Was 1999," 38; *Bison* (1983), 232.

29. *Bison* (1981), 38; Warren, "Unification and Collectiveness," 42. This is the first mention of the participation in the Greek show of Howard's chapter of Alpha Phi Omega, a national service organization based on scouting principles.

30. Walker, Jr., "Stepping Out," 62–63.

31. *Bison* (1981), 34.

32. *Bison* (1982), 42; *Bison* (1987), 43; *Bison* (1988), 38.

33. Bowen, "Showing Off," 62.

34. *Bison* (1986), 62; *Bison* (1988), 39.

35. Milner, "Homecoming Puts the Spotlight," 42.

36. Ibid., 42–43.

37. White, "Parading the Colors," 39; Cooper, "AKAs and Sigmas," B1; White, "Parading the Colors," 39.

38. White, "Parading the Colors," 39; Cooper, "AKAs and Sigmas," B1.

39. "Partying Like It Was 1999," 38.

40. Middleton interview.

41. Warren, "Unification and Collectiveness," 42; McLemore, "Metamorphosis," 62.

42. Samuels, "Probation prior to Vacation," 14–15.

43. Goldsborough, "Steppin' to a Higher Ground," 34.

44. Morris, "'Official' Step Shows Can Be Misleading," A2; Lee, "The Business of Steppin'," 28.

45. Francois, "Sounds of Thunder," 32.

46. Stalling, "Howard Students," A2; Berry, "Alpha Step Team," A4.

47. Martin, "High Steppin' Step Show," 29. The *Hilltop* coverage of the step show also reports on the mocking Alphas. See Presha, "Kappas, Zetas Out-Step Competition," A3. Mocking or marking uses nonverbal behavior to parody the steps or style of another group. For more on marking, see Mitchell-Kernan, "Signifying, Loud-talking, and Marking," 315–35.

48. Barrett, "Zetas Ask if Homecoming," C7; Robinson, "Omega Psi Phi," C7; "Homecoming—for Whom?" A6.

49. Woods, "Homecoming Step Show," A3; Shanks, "The Stompin' Ground," 39.

50. Harville interview; Payne, "Stepping Out on Campus," A8; Nomani, "Steeped in Tradition," A4; Freeman and Witcher, "Stepping into Black Power," 148; Davis interview; Jackson, "Blocking;" Cummings interview.

51. Brookins interview, 26 May 1995.

Chapter 2: A Ritual Dance of Identity

1. Transcription of videotape of "We Are the Brothers of Que Psi Phi," Alpha Chapter, Omega Psi Phi Fraternity Probate Show, 6 Apr. 1995, Howard University.

2. Freeman and Witcher, "Stepping into Black Power," 46; Herndon interview, 4 Feb. 2000.

3. Omega Psi Phi Web-site <http://www.omegapsiphifraternity.org> accessed on 29 March 2002; Sensabaugh interview.

4. Ford interview.

5. Dixon interview.

6. van Gennep, *Rites of Passage,* 2–3; Turner, "Anthropology of Performance," 101.

7. Turner, "Anthropology of Performance," 101; van Gennep, *Rites of Passage,* 11.

8. Cressey, "Death of a Black Fraternity," 1; Jones, "Inner Visions," 5.

9. Harris, "Place to Call Home," 14. For more on the effects of the membership intake process, see Jones, "Death before Dishonor."

10. Ford interview.

11. Ibid.

12. Kimbrough, "Black Greek 101 Dictionary," 2; Harris, "Place to Call Home," 13. For more on the culture of African American Greek-letter organizations, see Kimbrough, *Black Greek 101.*

13. Kimbrough, "Black Greek 101 Dictionary," 3.

14. Harris, "Place to Call Home," 13.

15. Joffe, "Student Conservatism at Howard," 2.

16. Odum, *Social and Mental Traits of the Negro,* 109, quoted in Malone, *Step-*

pin' on the Blues, 177; McGregory, "'There Are Other Ways to Get Happy,'" 286–88; and Frazier, *Black Bourgeoise,* 72. Little, in "The Extra-Curricular Activities of Black College Students," observes that at socials in the nineteenth century dancing was "at first prohibited. Instead, males and females marched in unison to music—the most intimate form of association permitted between the sexes at these affairs" (139).

17. Thompson, *African Art in Motion,* 45, 43.

18. Goodwin, "Sigma Sigma," 240; Ross, *The Divine Nine,* 448.

19. Turner, *Ritual Process,* 103; Taylor, "Hell-Week," 3.

20. Turner, *Ritual Process,* 96; Cummings interview.

21. Hall, *Dance of Life,* 10–11; Turner, *Ritual Process,* 136–40.

22. Yeats, "Among School Children," 136.

23. Turner, "Anthropology of Performance," 81.

24. Ibid., 74–75.

25. Terms for cracking vary. At Indiana University, students use the term *mauling* (Hodges, "Stepping," 15, 21). Branch, "Steppin' through These Hallowed Halls," 196.

26. Dixon interview; Iota Phi Theta, Inc., Web-site <http://www.iotaphitheta.org/faq.htm> accessed on 29 March 2002.

27. Dixon interview.

28. Ibid.

29. Videotape of Blue and White Weekend Step Show, 1985, University of Florida.

30. Abrahams, "Singing the Master," 101; Friedland, "Social Commentary," 146–50; Bell, *The World from Brown's Lounge,* 26; Mitchell-Kernan, "Signifying, Loud-talking, and Marking," 332–35.

31. Mitchell-Kernan, "Signifying, Loud-talking, and Marking," 332–35; for more on signifying, see Gates, *Signifying Monkey;* transcription of videotape of Alpha Phi Alpha block show, spring 1983, Virginia Tech.

32. Labov, "Rules for Ritual Insults," 265–314; transcription of videotape of Alpha Phi Alpha block show, spring 1983, Virginia Tech.

33. For more on metacommunication, see Babcock, "The Story in the Story"; Bateson, "A Theory of Play and Fantasy"; Jakobson, "Closing Statement"; and Turner, "Anthropology of Performance," 24.

34. Bauman, "Differential Identity," 31–41.

35. Alpha Kappa Alpha sorority member number one, interview, Blacksburg, Va.

36. Members of black sororities at the University of Southern Florida in Tampa were not familiar with the term *freaking;* they use *show dog* instead (Alpha Kappa Alpha interview, University of South Florida).

37. McGregory, "There Are Other Ways to Get Happy," 294; <http://www.Phillygreek.com> Web-site accessed on 9 July 1999.

38. McGregory, "There Are Other Ways to Get Happy," 302–3; Harris, "National Stepshow Competition."

39. McGregory, "There Are Other Ways to Get Happy," 300, 302.

40. Ibid., 305–6.

41. <http://www.Phillygreek.com> Web-site accessed on Aug. 1999.

42. Stuckey, *Going through the Storm,* 55, 59; Stearns and Stearns, *Jazz Dance,* 27–29; Douglass, *Life and Times,* 146. "Pinkster" derives from the Dutch word for "Pentecost" and was originally a celebration observed in the spring at Whitsuntide among Dutch immigrants in New York and in east New Jersey. By 1800 it was a predominantly African American festival. See Fabre, "Pinkster Festival," 13–28 for more on the celebration.

43. Stepping in Omega Psi Phi fraternity may have been influenced by the lindy hop. According to Stephon D. Henderson (interview 25 May 1995), stepping began "at the Rho Chi chapter at Tennessee State University—anywhere between 1941 and 1956" and "was called hopping there. Brothers at Tennessee State and in that middle Tennessee area still refer to it as hopping, because it was first referred to as hopping." A photograph captioned the "Omega Bop" in the 1969 *Bison* (221) shows Omega brothers standing on their right legs and kicking to the side in a movement reminiscent of the kicks done in the lindy hop. Rouverol ("'Hot,' 'Cool,' and 'Getting Down,'" 100) observes that the emphasis on unity, precision, and competition in tap, buck and wing, and chorus-line dancing "may have influenced stepping as we know it today." Other possible influences, she notes, "include cakewalking, and in recent years, even cheerleading and party walks." See Stearns and Stearns, *Jazz Dance,* 189–96, 123–24, and Malone, *Steppin' on the Blues,* for more on African American dance traditions.

44. Transcription of Alpha Phi Alpha block show, spring 1984, Virginia Tech.

45. Kochman, "Toward an Ethnography," 243; Brown, "Rap's Poem," 187–88; transcription of Alpha Phi Alpha block show, spring 1983, Virginia Tech.

46. For more on call and response, see Daniel and Smitherman, "How I Got Over," 26–39. Transcription of Alpha Phi Alpha block show, spring 1983, Virginia Tech.

47. The first quotation is from Friedland, "Social Commentary," 138; Alpha Kappa Alpha sorority member number one, interview; transcription of Alpha Kappa Alpha block show, spring 1986, Virginia Tech.

48. Cooke, "Nonverbal Communication," 33–43; transcription of Alpha Kappa Alpha block show, spring 1986, Virginia Tech.

49. Nomani, "Steeped in Tradition," A1.

Chapter 3: Stepping Out an African Heritage

1. Transcription of videotape, *A Christian Step Show and FUN-draiser,* 29 Mar. 1997, Theodore Roosevelt High School, Washington, D.C.; transcription from videotape by Fredrick Scott of Oak Grove Steppers, *Get Rid of the Garbage,* 30 Nov. 1994; transcription of videotape of *S.T.O.M.P.* competition, 1993; Alpha Kappa Alpha interview, University of South Florida; Alpha Kappa Alpha sorority member number one, interview.

2. Herskovits and Herskovits, *Dahomean Narrative,* 61.

3. Gordon interview.

4. Matthews interview.

5. Erlmann, *African Stars,* 99, quoting Tracey, *African Dances,* 7.

6. Erlmann, *African Stars,* 100, 145–47; Sumner, "African Quartette," n.p. There were no fraternities or sororities at Hampton Institute until 1947, but students at other colleges could have been exposed to his dancing.

7. Malone, *Steppin' on the Blues,* 247; Erlmann, *African Stars,* 100, 145–47; Semela interview.

8. Clifford, *Predicament of Culture,* 14; Johnson correspondence.

9. Northrup, *Twelve Years a Slave,* 219, quoted in Epstein, *Sinful Tunes,* 141; Paine, *Six Years in a Georgia Prison,* 179–80, quoted in Epstein, *Sinful Tunes,* 143.

10. Stearns and Stearns, *Jazz Dance,* 28; Thompson, *Four Moments,* 43, 28, 32.

11. Stearns and Stearns, *Jazz Dance,* 44–45. European influences on slave dances began earlier than the 1840s. Stearns and Stearns observe that many slaves were transported first to the West Indies, "leaving the slaves to become acclimatized before taking them to the mainland." There, "fashionable dances from the courts and elegant salons of Europe—Spanish, French, and English—became popular and were imitated by the slaves" (*Jazz Dance* 16–17).

12. Epstein, *Sinful Tunes,* 286; Stearns and Stearns, *Jazz Dance,* 30.

13. Forten, "Life on the Sea Islands," 594, quoted in Epstein, *Sinful Tunes,* 280. See also, Floyd, Jr., "Ring Shout!" 135–56.

14. Higginson, Diary, entry for 3 Dec. 1862, quoted in Epstein, *Sinful Tunes,* 280–81.

15. Thompson, "Aesthetic of the Cool," 88–96; Thompson, *African Art in Motion,* 5–45. Thompson interviewed ninety-four individuals from the Dan in Liberia; the Popo, Fon, and Yoruba of Dahomey; the Yoruba and Abakpa of Nigeria; the Banyang and Ejagham of Cameroon; the Kongo of Zaire; and migrant workers in Cameroon and Zaire.

16. Thompson, *African Art in Motion,* 6–7, 9.

17. Rouverol, "'Hot,' 'Cool,' and 'Getting Down,'" 104–6; Hinson, "When the Words," 396–421, quoted in Rouverol (104); Thompson, *African Art in Motion,* 9–10.

18. Thompson, *African Art in Motion,* 14; Overton R. Johnson Step Competition program, spring 1989, Virginia Tech.

19. Malone, *Steppin' on the Blues,* 192; Abrahams, *Singing the Master,* 93–94.

20. Transcription of videotape of Blue and White Weekend Step Show, 1985, University of Florida; Thompson, *African Art in Motion,* 14; Rouverol, "'Hot,' 'Cool,' and 'Getting Down,'" 105.

21. Thompson, *African Art in Motion,* 43.

22. Ibid., 44.

23. Ibid., 44–45.

24. Transcription of videotape by Teresa Torain of spring step show, 28 Apr. 1995,

Dietrich Dining Hall Courtyard, Virginia Tech; Malone, *Steppin' on the Blues,* 15, 16, 189; Thompson, "An Aesthetic of the Cool," 89–90.

25. Thompson, *African Art in Motion,* 16; Malone, *Steppin' on the Blues,* 209. Reacting to the difference in the costumes worn by the two rival sororities, Brooks ("'Steppin' Out,'" A4) criticizes AKA for choosing to wear dresses rather than what "should have been worn in a step show—*pants.*" Brooks also observes that "performers are supposed to 'step'—not sing or dance excessively" and criticizes other groups as well for too much singing. By the late 1980s, Malone notes (209), many sororities had begun to adopt fraternities' emphasis on fancy footwork, acrobatics, and hard stepping and so had begun stepping in pants or shorts rather than dresses. The idea that stepping should be different than singing and dancing was expressed in the Philadelphia Greek Picnic Stepshow on 24 June 1999 by AKA sisters from Old Dominion University, who proudly declared that they were not there to sing or dance but to step.

26. Videotape of Overton R. Johnson Step Competition, spring 1986, Virginia Tech.

27. Thompson, *African Art in Motion,* 18–24; Noches, "Stepping with Pride," A5, A8.

28. Malone, *Steppin' on the Blues,* 208.

29. Thompson, *African Art in Motion,* 18, 20; Pollitt, *Art and Experience,* 54–60.

30. Thompson, *African Art in Motion,* 20.

31. Transcription of videotape of Latino Greek Summer Step and Stroll Show, 1999, Roberto Clemente State Park, Bronx, N.Y.

32. Aldaño interview, 25 May 1999; transcriptions of videotapes of Overton R. Johnson Step Competition, spring 1986, Virginia Tech, and of Blue and White Weekend Step Show, 1985, University of Florida.

33. Thompson, *African Art in Motion,* 24; Jones and Hawes, *Step It Down,* 44, as quoted in Thompson, *African Art in Motion,* 24; Thompson, *African Art in Motion,* 24, 26.

34. Thompson, *African Art in Motion,* 30.

35. Thompson, "Aesthetic of the Cool," 94.

36. Thompson, *African Art in Motion,* 28; Davis, "'Deep in My Heart,'" 87.

37. Thompson, "Aesthetic of the Cool," 95–96; transcription by Jane Woodside of videotape of Dance Heritage Festival, 6 Apr. 1991, East Tennessee State University, Johnson City.

38. Davis, "'Deep in My Heart,'" 89, quoting Jones, *For the Ancestors,* 36–37.

39. Mitchell-Kernan, "Signifying, Loud-talking, and Marking"; Abrahams, "Black Talking on the Streets" and *Deep Down in the Jungle;* Jackson, *"Get Your Ass in the Water."*

40. Malone, *Steppin' on the Blues,* 172.

Chapter 4: Stepping Forth

1. Transcription of videotape, *A Christian Step Show and* FUN-*draiser,* 29 Mar. 1997, Theodore Roosevelt High School, Washington, D.C.

2. Ibid.

3. Freeman and Witcher, "Stepping into Black Power"; Nomani, "Steeped in Tradition"; Mercado-Valdes interview; Dezern, "Some Serious Stepping Out," D1.

4. Stalling, "Howard Students," A2; Gumbs interview; Upshaw interview; "Kirk Franklin . . . a Biography."

5. Petty interview. Simply Greek Online <http://www.simplygreek.com> lists upcoming step shows; <http://www.stepshow.com> and <http://www.stompshow.com> sell videotapes of step shows.

6. Brookins interview, 18 June 1996.

7. Terry interview.

8. Green interview; Martin, "Making a Joyful Noise," E6.

9. Ibid., E6.

10. Nance interview; Javetta and Geraldine Wiley interview.

11. Transcription of videotape, *A Christian Step Show and FUN-draiser,* 29 Mar. 1997, Theodore Roosevelt High School, Washington, D.C.

12. Petty and Smith interview.

13. Ibid.

14. Ibid.

15. Ibid.

16. Ibid.

17. Sumner interview.

18. Petty and Smith interview.

19. Iota Phi Theta Web-site <http://www.iotaphitheta.org/service.htm> accessed on 29 March 2002; Hudgens interview.

20. Hudgens interview.

21. Iota Phi Theta Web-site <http://www.iotaphitheta.org/service.htm> accessed on 12 April 2002.

22. Bates-Rudd, "Church Takes Higher Step," 4S; Ingram interview; Rodriguez, "One Step," 10.

23. Upshaw interview.

24. Transcription from videotape by Fredrick Scott of Oak Grove Steppers, *Get Rid of the Garbage,* 30 Nov. 1994.

25. Transcription from videotape by Fredrick Scott of Oak Grove Steppers, *The Oak Grove Steppers.*

26. Transcription from videotapes by Fredrick Scott Oak Grove Steppers, *Get Rid of the Garbage* and *The Oak Grove Steppers.*

27. Upshaw interview.

28. Ingram interview.

29. Gumbs interview; Mokhtar interview, 17 May 1996; transcription of videotape of Black Awareness Club Steppers, Blacksburg High School.

30. Gumbs interview.

31. Ibid.

32. Allen interview. The following information and quotations about the Gam-

ma Beta Tau Step Club in this section are from the Allen interview. For more on the Gamma Beta Tau Step Club, see their Web-site: <http://srwa.tripod.com/index.htm>.

33. Aldaño interviews, 31 July, 4 Aug. 1999.

34. Vargas interview; Fi Iota Alfa, Iota chapter at Oswego, Web-site <http://www.oswego.edu/~fia/history/body_history.html> accessed on 21 April 2002; Struck, "Latino Groups," 1999. Teams from the following organizations performed in the show: Alpha Rho Lambda Sorority, Sigma Iota Alpha Sorority, Lambda Pi Upsilon Sorority, Sigma Lambda Upsilon Sorority, Lambda Upsilon Lambda Fraternity, Omega Phi Chi Sorority, Omega Phi Beta Sorority, Sigma Lambda Beta Fraternity, and Lambda Theta Phi Fraternity.

35. Bahbahani interview.

36. Ibid.

37. For information on chapters, see Lambda Pi Upsilon national Web-site at <http://www.lpiu.com>, accessed on 21 April 2002.

38. Aldaño interviews, 25 May, 4 Aug. 1999; Lambda Upsilon Lambda Web-site <http://www.launidadlatina.org> accessed on 21 April 2002.

39. Aldaño interview, 25 May 1999.

40. Aldaño interview, 4 Aug. 1999.

41. Loza, *Tito Puente,* 8; Sanabria and Socolov, "Tito Puente: Long Live the King," 6, as quoted in Loza, *Tito Puente,* 8; Loza, *Tito Puente,* 8.

42. Crump, *Story of Kappa Alpha Psi,* 485–86.

43. Black and Latino Greek Council, West Chester University Web-site <http://iws.wcupa.edu/stu/blgc/> accessed on 29 March 2002.

44. Mercado-Valdes interview.

45. Nguyen interview. Sigma Phi Omega first organized at the University of Southern California in 1949 and has chapters in California and Texas and an affiliated fraternity called Beta Omega Phi.

46. Nguyen interview; Terry interview.

47. Kulkarni interview.

48. *Stagebill,* Kennedy Center, Washington, D.C., Jan. 2000, 29.

49. Williams interview.

50. Ibid.

51. Ibid.

52. Ibid.; Soweto Dance Theatre brochure, Jan. 2000.

53. Williams interview.

54. Williams interview; Woodruff interview; Williams interview; Woodruff, "Step Afrika!" B11.

55. Williams interview.

56. Rosenberg, *Can These Bones Live?* Lord, *Singer of Tales,* 30, 68; Foley, *Encyclopedia of American Folklore,* 449.

57. Brookins interview, 26 May 1995.

58. Transcription from videotape of *S.T.O.M.P.* competition, 1993.

59. Transcriptions of videotapes of spring block show, 1983, and Overton R. Johnson Step Competition, spring 1986, both at Virginia Tech.

60. Transcription of videotape, *A Christian Step Show and FUN-draiser,* 29 Mar. 1997, Theodore Roosevelt High School, Washington, D.C.; transcription of videotape by Fredrick Scott, *The Oak Grove Steppers;* transcription of videotape, *A Christian Step Show and* FUN-*draiser,* 29 Mar. 1997, Theodore Roosevelt High School, Washington, D.C.

61. This Alpha trade step was heard by Michael Herndon in Virginia in the mid–1970s (Herndon interview, 4 Feb. 2000). See Rose, *Black Noise,* 11–12, for the controversy surrounding Vanilla Ice's disputed composition of "Ice, Ice, Baby." Transcription by Jane Woodside of videotape of Dance Heritage Festival, 6 Apr. 1991, East Tennessee State University, Johnson City.

62. Transcription from videotape of *S.T.O.M.P.* competition, 1993.

63. Transcription of videotape of Blacksburg High School Black Awareness Club Steppers, 28 Feb. 1996; Jacinta Wiley interview; transcription of videotape, *A Christian Step Show and* FUN-*draiser,* 29 Mar. 1997, Theodore Roosevelt High School, Washington, D.C.

64. Transcription of videotape, *A Christian Step Show and FUN-draiser,* 29 Mar. 1997, Theodore Roosevelt High School, Washington, D.C.

Chapter 5: The Cultural Politics of African American Step Shows

1. My definition of cultural politics has been influenced by Whisnant, *All That Is Native and Fine.*

2. See Graham, *Our Kind of People,* 1–5, on brown bag and ruler tests.

3. Heintze, *Private Black Colleges in Texas,* 172, 169; Graham, *Our Kind of People,* 86.

4. Graham, *Our Kind of People,* 98. The term *Divine Nine* is from Ross, *Divine Nine.*

5. Graham, *Our Kind of People,* 89.

6. Ibid., 85.

7. Frazier, *Black Bourgeoisie,* 94–95.

8. Douglass, "What Are the Colored People?" 204–5, as cited in Gilroy, *Against Race,* 223.

9. Kilson, "Black Bourgeoisie Revisited," 90, 94, 93.

10. Thompson, *Black Elite,* xvi, 6, 159–60.

11. Ibid., 163, 165.

12. Landry, *New Black Middle Class,* 10; Benjamin, *Black Elite,* 32.

13. "Inter-fraternalism at Howard University"; "Interfraternity Council," 113.

14. "Greek Political Trust Smashed," 1; "Free-Swinging Student Council," 3.

15. Joffe, "Student Conservatism at Howard," 2.

16. Royster, "Omega Psi Phi Moves Forward," 6; Omega Psi Phi Web-site <http://www.omegapsiphifraternity.org> accessed on 29 March 2002.

17. Black, "'Why Do We Exist?'" 6.

18. Crump, *Story of Kappa Alpha Psi,* 457; Ross, *Divine Nine,* 49, 10, 11, 219, 136.

19. "Campus Speakout," 10–11; Cressey, "Death of a Black Fraternity," 1.

20. Holman, "Alphas Respond," 1, 5; Winfield, "Greek-letter 'Gangs,'" 2; St. Martin, "Frat: Slave Master Copycat," B9; Mills, "Wrongs of the Rites," B1, B6.

21. Madison, "Moving Past Greece to Africa," 9; Little, "Criticism Doesn't Sway," 12.

22. Malik Sigma Psi Web-site <http://www.geocities.com/terrible_taa/> accessed on 12 April 2002.

23. Berry, "African Greeks," 7. See Conway, "It's More Than Stepping," for a similar argument.

24. Hawthorne, "Greek Frats and Black Survival," letter to the editor, 4.

25. Brown, "Omega Psi Phi Disrupts," 4.

26. Hukumu, "Black 'Greeks' Confuse," 4.

27. Ferguson and Hailes, Jr., "Omega Psi Phi Expresses Pride," 4.

28. Ferguson and Hailes, Jr., "Following Is a Paid Advertisement," 10.

29. Chaney, *Fictions and Ceremonies,* 42. I prefer to use the term *respectability* because Chaney's term, *bourgeoisification,* is both awkward and objectionable to many African Americans who are sensitive to the charges of becoming bourgeois that Frazier and others have leveled at Greek-letter societies.

30. Transcription of videotape of Overton R. Johnson Step Competition, spring 1985, Virginia Tech.

31. Alpha Kappa Alpha sorority member number one, interview.

32. Transcription of videotape of block show, Dietrich Dining Hall Courtyard, spring 1986, Virginia Tech; Alpha Kappa Alpha sorority member number one, interview.

33. Alpha Kappa Alpha sorority member number one, interview; transcription of videotape of Overton R. Johnson Step Competition, spring 1986, Virginia Tech.

34. Transcription of videotape of Overton R. Johnson Step Competition, spring 1986, Virginia Tech.

35. Jamison interview.

36. Davis, "'Deep in My Heart,'" 85, 91; Alpha Kappa Alpha sorority member number two, interview.

37. Alpha Kappa Alpha sorority member number two, interview.

38. Harvin interview; notes from Kappa Alpha Psi step show, Southern Dance Traditions Conference, East Tennessee State University, Johnson City, 3 Mar. 1990.

39. National Pan-Hellenic Council Web-site <http://www.nphchq.org/resources> accessed on 20 April 2002. See also Ross, *Divine Nine,* 427–28.

40. Ross, *Divine Nine,* 428. At the First National Conference on Stepping, Blacksburg, Va., 6–7 Apr. 2001, panelists Michael Gordon, Lawrence Ross, Jerry Smith, Ishmail Conway, and Patricia Mason voiced the need to develop national and uniform standards for judging stepping competitions. According to Smith, sexually explicit routines and too much music are hurting the art form.

41. Ross, *Divine Nine*, 428.

42. Notes from Kappa Alpha Psi step show, Southern Dance Traditions Conference, East Tennessee State University, Johnson City, 3 Mar. 1990.

43. Matthews interview.

44. Davis, "'Deep in My Heart,'" 4.

45. Mercado-Valdes interview.

46. Brookins and Cotton interview.

47. Ibid.

48. Ibid.; Herndon interview, 4 Feb. 2000.

49. Williams interview.

50. Ibid.

51. Ibid.

52. Transcription of videotape of Step Afrika! USA step clinic, 22 Jan. 2000, Kennedy Center, Washington D.C.

53. Brookins and Cotton interview.

54. Upshaw interview.

55. Ross, *Divine Nine*, xii.

56. Rodriguez, "One Step at a Time," 8; Mercado-Valdes interview.

Epilogue

1. Henderson, *Understanding the New Black Poetry*, 44.

2. Ferguson and Hailes, "Following Is a Paid Advertisement," 10. In June 1998 a group of forty Augusta, Georgia, youths, the "No Limit Steppers," presented "Step Up and Step Away from Smoking," a program organized by the Art Factory, a community arts school, and funded by a $7,600 grant from the Georgia Department of Mental Health, Mental Retardation, and Substance Abuse. Wyatt, "Dance Show Dissuades Smoking."

3. Nomani, "Steeped in Tradition," A1.

Bibliography

Abrahams, Roger. "Black Talking on the Streets." In *Explorations in the Ethnography of Speaking*. Ed. Richard Bauman and Joel Sherzer, 240–62. New York: Cambridge University Press, 1974.

———. *Deep Down in the Jungle . . . : Negro Narrative Folklore from the Streets of Philadelphia*. Rev. ed. Chicago: Aldine Publishing, 1970.

———. *Singing the Master: The Emergence of African American Culture in the Plantation South*. New York: Pantheon, 1992.

Albright, Ann Cooper. *Choreographing Difference: The Body and Identity in Contemporary Dance*. Hanover: Wesleyan University Press/University Press of New England, 1997.

Austin, J. L. *How to Do Things with Words*. New York: Oxford University Press, 1965.

Babcock, Barbara A. "The Story in the Story: Metanarration in Folk Narrative." In *Verbal Art as Performance*. Ed. Richard Bauman, 61–80. Rowley, Mass.: Newbury House, 1972.

Barrett, Shaunda. "Zetas Ask if Homecoming Is Lost to Commercialism." *Hilltop*, 29 Oct. 1993, C7.

Bateson, Gregory. "A Theory of Play and Fantasy." In *Steps to an Ecology of Mind*, 177–93. New York: Ballantine, 1972.

Bates-Rudd, Rhonda. "Church Takes Higher Step to Relate to Younger Generation." *Detroit News*, 9 March 1995, 4S.

Bauman, Richard. "Differential Identity and the Social Base of Folklore." In *Toward New Perspectives in Folklore*. Ed. Américo Paredes and Richard Bauman, 31–41. Austin: University of Texas Press, 1972.

Bell, Michael J. *The World from Brown's Lounge: An Ethnography of Black Middle-Class Play*. Urbana: University of Illinois Press, 1983.

Benjamin, Lois. *The Black Elite: Facing the Color Line in the Twilight of the Twentieth Century*. Chicago: Nelson-Hall, 1991.

Berry, John. "African Greeks." *Hilltop*, 6 Oct. 1989, 7.

Berry, Stacy Bryan. "Alpha Step Team Journeys to South Africa." *Hilltop*, 20 Jan. 1995, A4.

Black and Latino Greek Council, West Chester University. Web-site at <http://iws.wcupa.edu/stu/blgc> accessed on 24 March 2002.

Black, Fred. "'Why Do We Exist?' Posed at Greek Weekend." *Hilltop*, 26 March 1965, 6.

Bowen, Sherri. "Showing Off." *Bison* (Howard University yearbook, 1985), 62–63.

Branch, Carol D. "Steppin' through These Hallowed Halls: Performance in African American Fraternities." Ph.D. diss., University of California, Los Angeles, 2001.

Brooks, Yvette. "'Steppin' Out to No Avail." *Collegiate Times*, 23 May 1986, A4.

Brown, H. Rap. "Rap's Poem." In *Understanding the New Black Poetry: Black Speech and Black Music as Poetic References.* Ed. Stephen Henderson, 187–88. New York: William Morrow, 1973.

Brown, Jacqueline. "Omega Psi Phi Disrupts Memorial Service." *Hilltop*, 29 Oct. 1976, 4.

"Campus Speakout." *Hilltop*, 8 March 1974, 10–11.

Clifford, James. *The Predicament of Culture: Twentieth-Century Ethnography, Literature, and Art.* Cambridge: Harvard University Press, 1988.

Conway, Ismail. "It's More Than Stepping: An Exploration of African-American Fraternities and Sororities." *Profile* (newsletter for NACA professional members), June 1991, 1–10.

Cooke, Benjamin G. "Nonverbal Communication among Afro-Americans: An Initial Classification." In *Rappin' and Stylin' Out: Communication in Urban Black America.* Ed. Thomas Kochman, 32–64. Urbana: University of Illinois Press, 1972.

Cooper, Lauren. "AKAs and Sigmas Take First Place at Annual Greek Show." *Hilltop*, 6 Nov. 1987, B1.

Cressey, Michael. "The Death of a Black Fraternity." *Hilltop*, 21 Feb. 1975, 1.

Crump, William L. *The Story of Kappa Alpha Psi: A History of the Beginning and Development of a College Greek Letter Organization, 1911–1983.* 3d ed. Philadelphia: Kappa Alpha Psi Fraternity, 1983.

Daniel, Jack L., and Geneva Smitherman. "How I Got Over: Communication Dynamics in the Black Community." *Quarterly Journal of Speech* 62 (1976): 26–39.

Davis, Amy. "'Deep in My Heart': Competition and the Function of Stepping in an African American Sorority." *North Carolina Folklore Journal* 43 (Summer–Fall 1996): 82–95.

Dezern, Craig. "Some Serious Stepping Out." *Orlando Sentinel*, 12 July 1993, D1–D2.

Douglass, Frederick. *Life and Times of Frederick Douglass, Written by Himself.* 1892 rev. ed. Reprint. New York: Macmillan, 1962.

———. "What Are the Coloured People Doing for Themselves?" In *African-American Social and Political Thought, 1850–1920.* Ed. Howard Brotz, 204–5. New Brunswick: Transaction Publishers, 1992.

Epstein, Dena J. *Sinful Tunes and Spirituals: Black Folk Music to the Civil War.* Urbana: University of Illinois Press, 1981.

Erlmann, Veit. *African Stars: Studies in Black South African Performance.* Chicago: University of Chicago Press, 1991.

Fabre, Geneviève. "Pinkster Festival, 1776–1811: An African-American Celebration." In *Feasts and Celebrations in North American Ethnic Communities*. Ed Ramón A.Gutiérrez and Geneviève Fabre, 1–28. Albuquerque: University of New Mexico Press, 1995.

Ferguson, K. Earl, and Edward Hailes, Jr. "Omega Psi Phi Expresses Pride in Fraternity." *Hilltop*, 12 Nov. 1976, 4.

———. "Following Is a Paid Advertisement." *Hilltop*, 12 Nov. 1976, 10.

Fi Iota Alfa. Phi Iota Alpha, Iota Chapter, SUNY at Oswego. Web-site at <http://www.oswego.edu/~fia/index.html> accessed on 20 April 2002.

Fine, Elizabeth C. "Oral-Formulaic Composition of African American Stepping." In *Oral Epic: Ethnic Traditions and Performance*. Vol. 1. Ed. O. Brytsyna and H. Douzhenok, 108–11. Kiev: Rylsky Institute of Art Studies, Folklore and Ethnology, National Academy of Sciences, 1997.

———. "Stepping, Saluting, Cracking, and Freaking: The Cultural Politics of African American Step Shows." *The Drama Review* 35 (1991): 39–59.

Floyd, Samuel A., Jr. "Ring Shout! Literary Studies, Historical Studies, and Black Music Inquiry." In *Signifyin(g), Sanctifyin', and Slam Dunking: A Reader in African American Expressive Culture*. Ed. Gena Dagel Caponi, 135–56. Amherst: University of Massachusetts Press, 1999.

Foley, John Miles. "Lord, Albert Bates (1912–1991)." In *American Folklore: An Encyclopedia*. Ed. Jan Harold Brunvand, 449–50. New York: Garland Publishing, 1996.

Forten, Charlotte L. "Life on the Sea Islands," 13 May 1864, 587–96. Quoted in Dena J. Epstein, *Sinful Tunes and Spirituals: Black Folk Music to the Civil War*, 280. Urbana: University of Illinois Press, 1981.

Foster, Susan Leigh. *Reading Dancing: Bodies and Subjects in Contemporary American Dance*. Berkeley: University of California Press, 1986.

Francois, Margarita. "Sounds of Thunder: Black Greeks Step for Championship Title." *Bison* (Howard University yearbook, 1993), 32.

Frazier, E. Franklin. *Black Bourgeoisie: The Rise of a New Middle Class in the United States*. New York: Free Press, 1962.

Freeman, Marilyn, and Tina Witcher. "Stepping into Black Power." *Rolling Stone*, 24 March 1988, 143–53.

"Free-Swinging Student Council Takes over May, Grid, Hilltop Voting: Greeks Go Underground." *Hilltop*, 17 March 1953, 3.

Friedland, Lee Ellen. "Social Commentary in African-American Movement Performance." In *Human Action Signs in Cultural Context: The Visible and the Invisible in Movement and Dance*. Ed. Brenda Farnell, 136–57. Metuchen: Scarecrow Press, 1995.

Gamma Beta Tau Step Club. Web-site at <http://srwa.tripod.com/index.htm> accessed on 22 April 2002.

Gates, Henry Louis. *Signifying Monkey: A Theory of Afro-American Literary Criticism*. Cambridge: Oxford University Press, 1988.

Giles, Leroy E. "Greeks Ignore Debate Invitation." *Hilltop* 24 April 1964, 2.

Gilroy, Paul. *Against Race: Imagining Political Culture beyond the Color Line.* Cambridge: Harvard University Press, 2000.

Goldsborough, Angel. "Steppin' to a Higher Ground, Greek Show." *Bison* (Howard University yearbook, 1991), 34.

Goodwin, Ruby Berkely. "Sigma Sigma." In Pearl Schwartz White, *Behind These Doors—A Legacy: The History of Sigma Gamma Rho Sorority.* Ed. Lillie Wilkes, 240. Chicago: Sigma Gamma Rho Sorority, 1974.

Graham, Lawrence Otis. *Our Kind of People: Inside America's Black Upper Class.* New York: HarperCollins, 1999.

"Greek Political Trust Smashed." *Hilltop,* 17 March 1953, 1.

Hall, Edward T. *The Dance of Life: The Other Dimension of Time.* New York: Doubleday, 1983.

Harris, Rita. "National Stepshow Competition to be Held at the Twenty-fifth Aniversary of the Philadelphia Greek Picnic." Simply Greek, Inc. Web-site at <http://www.Phillygreek.com> accessed on 9 July 1999.

Harris, Tina M. "A Place to Call Home: The System of Communication among African American Sorority Members on a Predominantly White College Campus." Presented at the eighty-third National Communication Association Conference, Chicago. Ill., Nov. 1977.

Hawthorne, Vance. "Greek Frats and Black Survival." *Hilltop,* 5 March 1976, 4.

Heintze, Michael R. *Private Black Colleges in Texas, 1865–1954.* College Station: Texas A&M University Press, 1985.

Henderson, Stephen. *Understanding the New Black Poetry: Black Speech and Black Music as Poetic References.* New York: William Morrow, 1973.

Herskovits, Melville, and Frances Herskovits. *Dahomean Narrative: A Cross-Cultural Approach.* Evanston: Northwestern University Press, 1958.

Higginson, Thomas Wentworth. Diary entry for 3 Dec. 1862. Ms. Houghton Library, Harvard University. Quoted in Dena J. Epstein, *Sinful Tunes and Spirituals: Black Folk Music to the Civil War,* 280–81. Urbana: University of Illinois Press, 1981.

Hinson, Glenn. "When the Words Roll and the Fire Flows: Spirit, Style, and Experience in African American Gospel Performance." Ph.D. diss., University of Pennsylvania, 1989. Quoted in Alicia J. Rouverol, "'Hot,' 'Cool,' and 'Getting Down': African American Style and Aesthetics in Stepping." *North Carolina Folklore Journal* 43 (Summer–Fall 1996): 96–108.

Hodges, Lydia. "Stepping: Dancing for Cultural Expression through Precision and Synchronization." *Indiana Daily Student,* 1 Nov. 1991, 15, 21.

Holman, E. K. "The Alphas Respond." *Hilltop,* 28 Feb. 1975, 1, 5.

"Homecoming—for Whom?" *Hilltop,* 5 Nov. 1995, A6.

Hukumu, Kujaliwa. "Black 'Greeks' Confuse Identity and Purpose of Self-Images." *Hilltop,* 5 Nov. 1976, 4.

"Inter-fraternalism at Howard University." *Bison* (Howard University yearbook, 1930), n.p.

"The Inter-fraternity Council." *Bison* (Howard University yearbook, 1932), 113.

Iota Phi Theta. Web-site at <http://www.iotaphitheta.org> accessed on 20 April 2002.

Jackson, Bruce. *"Get Your Ass in the Water and Swim Like Me": Narrative from Black Oral Tradition.* Cambridge: Harvard University Press, 1974.

Jackson, Florence M. "Blocking: A General Overview." Unpublished mss. Virginia Tech, 1984.

Jakobson, Roman. "Closing Statement: Linguistics and Poetics." In *Style in Language.* Ed. T. A. Sebeok, 350–77. New York: John Wiley and Sons, 1960.

Joffe, Carole. "Student Conservatism at Howard." *Hilltop,* 9 April 1965, 2. Reprinted from *The Justice* (Brandeis University), 16 March 1965.

Johnson, John. "It's Greek Time Again." *Hilltop,* 9 Feb. 1973, 6.

Jones, Bessie. *For the Ancestors: Autobiographical Memories.* Urbana: University of Illinois Press, 1983. Quoted in Amy Davis, "'Deep in My Heart': Competition and the Function of Stepping in an African American Sorority." *North Carolina Folklore Journal* 43 (Summer–Fall 1996): 82–95.

Jones, Ricky L. "Death before Dishonor: De-Politicalization and the Failure of Black Greek Leadership to Address Its Internal Threat to Black Life." In *Reflections on the Leadership Crisis in the Black Experience: An Interdisciplinary Perspective.* Ed. Terry Kershaw and Charles Jones. Albany: SUNY Press, in press.

Jones, Steven R. "Inner Visions: Taking Exception: Another Commentary on the Black Fraternity and the Concept of Pledging." *Hilltop,* 28 Feb. 1975, 5.

Kilson, Martin. "The Black Bourgeoisie Revisited: From E. Franklin Frazier to the Present." *Dissent* 30 (Winter 1983): 85–96.

Kimbrough, Walter M. *Black Greek 101: The Culture, Customs, and Challenges of Historically Black Fraternities and Sororities.* Madison: Fairleigh Dickinson University Press, in press.

———. "Black Greek 101 Dictionary." Photocopy. Rev. April 1998. Old Dominion University, Norfolk, Va.

"Kirk Franklin—a Biography." Web-site at <http://www.nunation.com/bio.html> rev. 14 April 2000.

Kochman, Thomas. "Toward an Ethnography of Black American Speech Behavior." In *Rappin' and Stylin' Out: Communication Behavior in Urban Black America.* Ed. Thomas Kochman, 241–64. Urbana: University of Illinois Press, 1972.

Labov, William. "Rules for Ritual Insults." In *Rappin' and Stylin' Out: Communication in Urban Black America,* ed. Thomas Kochman, 265–314. Urbana: University of Illinois Press, 1972.

Lambda Upsilon Lambda. Web-site at <http://www.launidadlatina.org> accessed on 21 April 2002.

Landry, Bart. *The New Black Middle Class.* Berkeley: University of California Press, 1987.

Lee, Donna. "The Business of Steppin'." *Bison* (Howard University yearbook, 1992), 28.

Little, Monroe H. "The Extra-Curricular Activities of Black College Students, 1868–1940." *Journal of Negro History* 65 (Spring 1980): 135–48.

Little, Rebecca. "Criticism Doesn't Sway New Fraternity, KMT." *Hilltop,* 3 Nov. 1989, 3, 12.

Lord, Albert Bates. *The Singer of Tales.* Cambridge: Harvard University Press, 1964.

Loza, Steven. *Tito Puente and the Making of Latin Music.* Urbana: University of Illinois Press, 1999.

Madison, Chris. "Moving Past Greece to Africa." *Hilltop,* 1 Dec. 1989, 9.

Malik Sigma Psi. Web-site at <http://www.geocities.com/terrible_taa/> accessed on 12 April 2002.

Malone, Jacqui. *Steppin' on the Blues: The Visible Rhythms of African American Dance.* Urbana: University of Illinois Press, 1996.

Martin, James. "High Steppin' Step Show." *Bison* (Howard University yearbook, 1994), 29.

Martin, Norma. "Making a Joyful Noise." *Austin American Statesman,* 21 June 1999, E1, E6.

McGregory, Jerrilyn M. "'There Are Other Ways to Get Happy': African-American Urban Folklore." Ph.D. diss., University of Pennsylvania, 1992.

McLemore, Mignon. "Metamorphosis." *Bison* (Howard University yearbook, 1986), 62.

Mills, David. "The Wrongs of the Rites of Brotherhood: Leaders of Black Fraternities Move to End a Cruel Tradition of Violent Hazing." *Washington Post,* 18 June 1990, B1, B6.

Milner, Sherri. "Homecoming Puts the Spotlight on Greek Showoffs." *Bison* (Howard University yearbook, 1987), 42.

Mitchell-Kernan, Claudia. "Signifying, Loud-Talking, and Marking." In *Rappin' and Stylin' Out: Communication in Black America.* Ed. Thomas Kochman, 315–35. Urbana: University of Illinois Press, 1972.

Morris, Sonja. "'Official' Step Shows Can Be Misleading." *Hilltop,* 25 Oct. 1991, A2.

"Negro Group Initiates Two White Women." *Washington Post,* 30 Nov. 1949. Howard University Vertical Files, "Alpha Kappa Alpha."

Nelson, Jill. "Stepping Lively: At Black Frats and Sororities, the Dance That Unites." *Washington Post,* 29 May 1990, C1, 8–9.

Ness, Sally Ann. *Body, Movement and Culture: Kinesthetic and Visual Symbolism in a Philippine Community.* Philadelphia: University of Pennsylvania Press, 1992.

Noches, Lucinda. "Stepping with Pride: Contest Raises Funds for Scholarship." *Collegiate Times,* 26 May 1987, A5, A8.

Nomani, Asra Q. "Steeped in Tradition, 'Step Dance' Unites Blacks on Campus." *Wall Street Journal,* 10 July 1989, A1, A4.

Northup, Solomon. *Twelve Years a Slave: The Narrative of Solomon Northup, a Citizen of New York, Kidnapped in Washington City in 1841 and Rescued in 1853, from a Cotton Plantation near the Red River in Louisiana.* Auburn, N.Y.: Derby and Miller, 1853.

Novack, Cynthia J. *Sharing the Dance: Contact Improvisation and American Culture.* Madison: University of Wisconsin Press, 1990.

Odum, Howard W. *Social and Mental Traits of the Negro: Research into the Conditions of the Negro Race in Southern Towns: A Study in Race Traits, Tendencies, and Prospects.* 1910. Reprint. New York: AMS Press, 1968.

Omega Psi Phi Fraternity, Inc. Web-site at <http:// www.omegapsiphifraternity.org> accessed on 20 April 2002.

Paine, Lewis W. *Six Years in a Georgia Prison, Narrative of Lewis W. Paine, Who Suffered Imprisonment Six Years in Georgia, for the Crime of Aiding the Escape of a Fellowman from the State, after He Had Fled from Slavery. Written by Himself.* New York: Printed for the Author, 1851. Quoted in Dena J. Epstein, *Sinful Tunes and Spirituals: Black Folk Music to the Civil War,* 143. Urbana: University of Illinois Press, 1981.

"Partying Like It Was 1999!" *Bison* (Howard University yearbook, 1983), 38–39.

Payne, Melinda J. "Stepping Out on Campus." *Roanoke Times and World News,* 15 Oct. 1987, A1, A8.

Pollitt, J. J. *Art and Experience in Classical Greece.* New York: Cambridge University Press, 1972.

Presha, Janet. "Kappas, Zetas Out-Step Competition to Bring Home Cham[p]ionship Title." *Hilltop,* 5 Nov. 1993, A3.

Rich, Paul. "Freemasonry, the Greeks, and Stepping." Presented at the First National Conference on Stepping, 6–7 Apr. 2001, Virginia Tech, Blacksburg.

Robinson, Tushon. "Omega Psi Phi: Homecoming Away from 'Home' Destroys the Aura." *Hilltop,* 29 Oct. 1993, C7.

Rodriguez, Cindy. "One Step at a Time." *Boston Globe,* 7 July 1996, 8, 10.

Rosenberg, Bruce A. *Can These Bones Live? The Art of the American Folk Preacher.* Rev. ed. Chicago: University of Illinois Press, 1988.

Rose, Tricia. *Black Noise: Rap Music and Black Culture in Contemporary America.* Hanover: Wesleyan University Press/University Press of New England, 1994.

Ross, Lawrence. *The Divine Nine: The History of African American Fraternities and Sororities.* New York: Kensington Books, 2000.

Rouverol, Alicia J. "'Hot,' 'Cool,' and 'Getting Down': African American Style and Aesthetics in Stepping." *North Carolina Folklore Journal* 43 (Summer–Fall 1996): 96–108.

Royster, Don. "Omega Psi Phi Moves Forward." *Hilltop,* 26 March 1965, 6.

Samuels, Karen. "Probation prior to Vacation." *Bison* (Howard University yearbook, 1988), 14–15.

Sanabria, Bobby, and Ben Socolov. "Tito Puente: Long Live the King." *Hip: Highlights in Percussion for the Percussion Enthusiast* 5 (Spring–Summer): 1–7, 22–23. Quoted in Steven Loza, *Tito Puente and the Making of Latin Music,* 8. Urbana: University of Illinois Press, 1999.

Scott, Fredrick. *Get Rid of the Garbage.* Video recording of Rev. Mark Thomas, Oak Grove A.M.E. Church, Detroit, Mich., 30 Nov. 1994.

———. *The Oak Grove Steppers.* Video recording of selected performances. 1996.

Shanks, S. Christina. "The Stompin' Ground." *Bison* (Howard University yearbook, 1995), 39.

Smith, Kym. "Why Walk in a Line?" *Bison* (Howard University yearbook, 1982), 30.

Stalling, Chelsea L. "Howard Students Scheduled to Display Talents in Clinton's Inaugural Festivities." *Hilltop*, 15 Jan. 1993, A2.

Stearns, Marshall, and Jean Stearns. *Jazz Dance: The Story of American Vernacular Dance*. New York: Schirmer Books, 1968.

St. Martin, Jude, Jr. "Frat: Slave Master Copycat." *Hilltop*, 23 Sept. 1994, B9.

Struck, Carla. "Latino Groups Expand Greek Life on College Campuses." Hispanic Link News Service, Washington, D.C.

Stuckey, Sterling. *Going through the Storm: The Influence of African American Art in History*. New York: Oxford University Press, 1994.

Sumner, Dwight. "African Quartette on School Campaign." *Hampton Script*, 30 Sept. 1931, n.p.

Taylor, Van. "Hell-Week." *Hilltop*, 25 Nov. 1925, 3.

Thompson, Daniel C. *A Black Elite: A Profile of Graduates of UNCF Colleges*. Contributions in Afro-American and African Studies no. 98. Westport: Greenwood Press, 1986.

Thompson, Robert Farris. "An Aesthetic of the Cool: West African Dance." *African Forum* 2 (Fall 1966): 85–102.

———. *African Art in Motion: Icon and Act*. Los Angeles: University of California Press, 1979.

———. *The Four Moments of the Sun: Kongo Art in Two Worlds*. Washington, D.C.: National Gallery of Art, 1981.

Tracey, Hugh. *African Dances of the Witwaterstrand Gold Mines*. Johannesburg: African Music Society, 1952. Quoted in Veit Erlmann, *African Stars: Studies in Black South African Performance*, 99. Chicago: University of Chicago Press, 1991.

Turner, Victor. "The Anthropology of Performance." In *The Anthropology of Performance*. Ed. Victor Turner, 72–98. New York: PAJ Publications, 1986.

———. *The Ritual Process: Structure and Anti-Structure*. Ithaca: Cornell University Press, 1969.

van Gennep, Arnold. *Rites of Passage*. Chicago: University of Chicago Press, 1960.

Walker, James L., Jr. "Stepping Out: African-American Feet Beat Out a Greek Message." *Bison* (Howard University yearbook 1990), 62–63.

Warren, Robert. "Unification and Collectiveness." *Bison* (Howard University yearbook, 1982), 42–43.

Wesley, Charles H. *The History of Alpha Phi Alpha: A Development in Negro College Life*. 1920, 1950. Rev. ed. Chicago: Foundation Publishers, 1991.

Whisnant, David. *All That Is Native and Fine: The Politics of Culture in an American Region*. Chapel Hill: University of North Carolina Press, 1983.

White, Andrea. "Parading the Colors of Their Respective Sororities and Fraternities, Campus Greeks Showed Their Pride while Stepping Out!" *Bison* (Howard University yearbook, 1988), 39.

Winfield, George. "Greek-Letter 'Gangs' in Perspective." *Hilltop,* 20 Oct. 1989, 2.

Woodruff, Paul. "Step Afrika!" *Hilltop,* 17 Nov. 1995, B11.

Woods, Aubaine. "Homecoming Step Show Faces Organization Boycott." *Hilltop,* 16 Sept. 1994, A3.

Wyatt, Kristen. "Dance Show Dissuades Smoking." *Augusta Chronicle,* 20 June, 1998, metro ed. Web-site at <http://augustachronicle.com/stories/062098/met_124–4342.shtml> accessed on 20 April 2002.

Yarger, Lisa J. "'That's . . . Where Stepping Came From': Afrocentricity and Beliefs about Stepping." *North Carolina Folklore Journal* 43 (Summer–Fall 1996): 109–19.

Yeats, W. B. "Among School Children." In *Chief Modern Poets of England and America,* vol. 1: *The British Poets.* 4th ed. Ed. Gerald DeWitt Sanders, John Herbert Nelson, and M. L. Rosenthal, 135–36. New York: Macmillan, 1962.

Index

Elizabeth C. Fine is an associate professor in the Center for Interdisciplinary Studies at Virginia Tech, with a joint appointment in the Department of Communication Studies. Her research is in the areas of performance studies, folklore, and communication. She holds a Ph.D. in communication from the University of Texas at Austin. She is author of *The Folklore Text: From Performance to Print* and coeditor of *Performance, Culture, and Identity.*

The University of Illinois Press
is a founding member of the
Association of American University Presses.

Composed in 10/13 Sabon
with Helvetica Neue display
by Jim Proefrock
at the University of Illinois Press
Manufactured by Thomson-Shore, Inc.

University of Illinois Press
1325 South Oak Street
Champaign, IL 61820-6903
www.press.uillinois.edu